THE MYSTERIES REVEALED

Other Titles From New Falcon Publications

Sex and Drugs
Prometheus Rising
The New Inquisition
    By Robert Anton Wilson
Rebels and Devils
    Edited by C. S. Hyatt; with William S. Burroughs, et. al.
Undoing Yourself With Energized Meditation
Secrets of Western Tantra
The Tree of Lies
    By Christopher S. Hyatt, Ph.D.
Pacts With The Devil
    By S. J. Black and Christopher. S. Hyatt, Ph.D.
Urban Voodoo
    By Christopher. S. Hyatt, Ph.D. and S. J. Black
Eight Lectures on Yoga
Gems From the Equinox
    By Aleister Crowley
Neuropolitique
Info-Psychology
Game of Life
    By Timothy Leary, Ph.D.
Zen Without Zen Masters
    By Camden Benares
The Complete Golden Dawn System of Magic
What You Should Know About the Golden Dawn
    By Israel Regardie
Metaskills: The Feeling Art of Therapy
    By Amy Mindell, Ph.D.
Astrology and Consciousness: The Wheel of Light
    By Rio Olesky
Carl Sagan and Immanuel Velikovsky
    By Charles Ginenthal
Soul Magic: Understanding Your Journey
    By Katherine Torres, Ph.D.

And to get your free catalog of *all* of our titles, write to:
NEW FALCON PUBLICATIONS
Catalog Dept.
1739 East Broadway Road, Suite 1-277
Tempe, AZ 85282 U.S.A.

THE MYSTERIES REVEALED

A Handbook of Esoteric Psychology,
Philosophy and Spirituality

By

Andrew Schneider

1995
NEW FALCON PUBLICATIONS
TEMPE, ARIZONA U.S.A.

International Standard Book Number: 1-56184-124-2

First Edition 1995

Cover art by S. Jason Black

The paper used in this publication meets the minimum require-ments of the American National Standard for Permanence of Paper for Printed Library Materials Z39.48-1984

Address all inquiries to:
New Falcon Publications
1739 East Broadway Road Suite 1-277
Tempe, Arizona 85282 U.S.A.
(or)
1605 East Charleston Blvd.
Las Vegas, NV 89104 U.S.A.

ACKNOWLEDGMENTS

I wish to extend my sincerest appreciation to those special people who have assisted me in the process of bringing this Teaching to you, the reader. For their time, energy and care, I thank Jean Bryson, Peter Duryea, Gayle Konkle, Zoe Thompson, Frances Moore and the wonderful people at New Falcon. My greatest indebtedness is to my wife Bonnie, who has spent hundreds of hours typing my writing and dictation, and retyping all my revisions.

I also wish to acknowledge with gratitude the many people who have honored me with their presence in my lectures and workshops over the past twenty years, where I have had the opportunity of developing and teaching much of the content of this book.

Words fail when it comes to expressing adequately the gratitude I feel toward all my teachers of The Teaching—the invisible, compassionate Ones who inspire and guide us so beautifully, and the many writers who, like myself, have struggled t o express the inexpressible. To all of you, my humble thanks.

TABLE OF CONTENTS

INTRODUCTION

This book has been written for every sincere individual who is interested in understanding him/herself and the purpose and meaning of life.

The knowledge I have about the nature of life has been derived from a tradition that is at least as old as Humanity itself and has been available to anyone who is intuitive enough to perceive it or mentally alert enough to receive it. The knowledge found in these pages is part of the 'Ancient Wisdom', also referred to as the 'Mysteries', the 'Ageless Wisdom', the 'Wisdom Teachings', or simply 'The Teaching'. I have, of course, filtered it through my understanding and expressed it in my words.

This teaching does not originate in words, books or even sacred treatises. It originates as lives lived on higher planes of existence. When these lives of great beings reveal themselves through expression on lower planes (such as in the human kingdom), or when the lower contacts the higher, then purpose and meaning are revealed. This revelation is usually understood as universal laws or principles, and human beings then formulate the experience into words. *The mysteries are thus revealed.*

Words are useful as expressions of concepts, but may equally hide or reveal aspects of truth, beauty or goodness. If the words and concepts point the way to a more inclusive, broader experience of life then they serve well. If they are taken literally and as ultimate Reality in themselves then it is not Reality which is experienced but a limited form of Reality appropriately called *illusion.*

We all live in illusion, but sometimes break through into glimpses and experiences of what is Real. The Real is simply the bigger picture of life, the level of causes producing the effects with which we usually identify.

Any lack of understanding or limitation is either a distortion or but the smaller picture isolated from the larger; it is an effect unrelated to the cause. As we attempt to understand ourselves and life we become involved in two phases of a process:

—We willingly let go of our perceptions that have been created by past conditioning and limited concepts, and

—We open ourselves to experience the whole of which we are a part. This opening to the whole is an adventure into the wonderful mystery of life.

This book presents vital aspects of that whole so that we can begin to relate to it more fully, more intelligently and more lovingly, and become more of who we really are. This is a process of becoming whole, fulfilling our purpose, living meaningfully and being real.

These teachings are for everyone, regardless of race, creed or color, but not everyone is prepared to follow them as a way of life. There is a purpose to everyone's life and it is that purpose, known or unknown, which dictates our inclinations, interests and pursuits. Everyone wants to be happy because happiness is the usual feeling that we experience when our purpose is being fulfilled. When that purpose is conscious and we are living it then *joy* replaces happiness as a deeper experience of fulfillment.

There are many paths that people can pursue in their quest for happiness or joy. Their life's purpose will incline them towards one of these:

—There is the *physical path* which usually involves physical work and physical relating of one sort or another; it often leads a person into a deeper knowledge of physical laws and the laws of external nature.

—The *mystic path* is the next stage wherein a person is involved with the emotional life and its transmutation into expression through the heart. Here a person learns the rudiments of feeling and loving relationships. Followers of this path are usually called 'devotees' or 'religious'.

—The *occult path* leads to the development, expression and control of the mind and teaches a person the mental laws that influence and determine physical and emotional realities.

—Finally, there is the *esoteric path* which involves the integration of heart and mind while going one step further into the realm of Soul and Spirit. It is on this path that life transcends the personal while totally encompassing it. The Esoteric Path is the essence of all viable paths to self-actualization and to unity with the Divine. It is not contradictory to any other path and, in fact, elucidates all others. It is universal, inclusive and comprehensive. This book is an expression of the esoteric path.

In every person's evolution there comes a time when the mind needs to be developed. This happens when an individual realizes that he/she is not the victim of circumstances or a puppet on a string, but has the potential to direct and control his/her life. Developing the mind enables a person to take charge of the emotions, to create consciously one's experiences, and to connect with the source of love, power and understanding within.

Mind is the bridge in consciousness and the revealer of meaning. If one is attempting to discover the 'why?' of life and experience, the developed mind will reveal the answers. Mind is the vehicle through which Joy can be experienced, Power can be expressed, and Unconditional Love can become a reality.

The esoteric approach does develop the *mind* but it is not the mind of cold reason; it is the higher mind of discernment and spiritual discrimination; it is a loving mind.

The esoteric way places greater emphasis, however, on developing the *intuition* which is beyond the mind itself. Intuition is not to be confused with ordinary psychic ability. The intuition enables a person to perceive and relate to universal Unity, Truth, Goodness and Beauty in all of their many aspects, and to understand how these realities can be practically expressed and implemented in personal life and society.

Another emphasis in the esoteric approach is the development of the *heart*—not the emotional heart, for that is already developed in most people, but the intelligent intuitive heart, which is the vehicle of intelligent love and compassion.

The union of heart (love) and head (understanding) produces WISDOM, the true essence of Soul. Esoteric work is aimed at developing and expressing this wisdom. This is why the esoteric teaching is often called the Wisdom Teachings or the Ancient Wisdom.

PART 1

THE GREAT WORK

I

WHAT IS ESOTERICISM?

The word 'esoteric' simply means that which is inner, contrasted with that which is outer or 'exoteric.' Esotericism is therefore the body of knowledge or wisdom about all aspects of life which are within, behind or beyond the outer appearance, form or expression of life's many aspects.

True knowledge or wisdom is not something we can acquire solely by using our minds and brains, learning it in an academic way. It can only be gained by experience. Experience does not imply doing something physically, but rather necessitates a direct contact between one's consciousness and a state of energy. For example, if you meet someone who has just suffered a severe loss and you attune to that person, feeling what they feel, you have an experience that can make you a wiser person, knowing more about the nature of loss and its consequent pain. If, however, you are able to experience that person at a deeper level of being, you will gain the wisdom of knowing the real purpose of the loss and its meaning in that person's life. To have this deeper experience requires the ability to have conscious awareness of Soul, or Higher Self. To take this example even further, if you have conscious awareness of the Planetary Soul you would be able to experience the person's loss in the light of all losses that everyone experiences and see what place loss has in the unfolding intelligent and loving life of the planet. The wisdom derived from such experience would be very profound.

What is esoteric cannot, as you see, be neatly and simply defined or confined to narrow parameters. There are many levels of what is inner, and many dimensions of energy states that can be experienced.

Behind every phenomenon exists a 'world' of energies. It is energy which produces phenomena or forms when it descends or manifests in the lower three worlds of thought, feeling and physical matter. Beyond these worlds are other formless but real worlds or dimensions of life energy.

All of that which exists is some type of energy that has its source in ultimate simplicity or purity of formless energy. For reasons beyond our comprehension we perceive this simple energy manifesting itself by degrees in greater complexity. As it does so it descends through many levels of expression, first formless and then formed. When it is formed we experience it with our form nature—our bodies, emotions and brain-minds. When it is still formless we can, however, also experience it with the formless aspects of our individual consciousness—namely our higher minds, intuition, Soul and Spirit.

Every stepping down of energy from a higher (simpler and more inclusive) state to a lower (more complex and particular/exclusive) state is cause-producing-effect. It is the higher state of energy, being cause, that is the *purpose* and *meaning* of every lower state or effect. If we do not relate to or search for the cause, if we do not attempt to experience beyond phenomena, we cannot know the higher purpose or meaning of anything, least of all ourselves.

It is also this level of cause which is the *quality* of a thing or person. *Quantity* is a measure of the outer characteristics, such as size, physical features, weight, etc. *Quality* is an indication of the energy which produces the form. It is through the experience of quality that we are able to direct energy, including our own, and actually become it to the point where we are able to function as conscious causes rather than unconscious effects of life. This ability enhances our power, enables us to love unconditionally and opens the door to true understanding.

What makes us who we are is our individuality. We usually equate our individuality with our personality (physical body, emotions, brain-mind). The personality is but the outer or exoteric expression of individuality. The Soul is the inner or esoteric expression of individuality. Being esoteric it is of a higher energy state—more inclusive, more creative and causative, and therefore more real and central to our being.

As consciously aware Soul beings, we can and do serve in our capacities as Redeemers, Saviors and Interpreters. We function as the mediating principle between higher and lower, bringing the energies from higher sources down to earth, anchoring and grounding them. We relate the formless causes to the formed effects; we embrace the form worlds as meaningful creations of our unconditional love, and we bring clarity and purpose to all that happens.

The principal means whereby the higher energies are grounded is by incorporating them consciously in ourselves and expressing them through our thoughts, feelings and actions as virtues and qualities of being, such as kindness, sharing, sacrifice, discipline, unconditional love, forgiveness, acceptance, patience, etc.—in short, all quality reflective of truth, goodness and beauty, producing ever-increasing oneness or unity.

Esotericism as a way of life is an art. It is the art of living from the inner reaches of one's being. As art it is based on sensitive, intuitive perception, open to inspiration. And as true art it is a creative way of being, expressive of true universality. But it is also a science—a science of the soul of things. It has its own terminology, methods of procedure and laws. Esoteric science, for example, reasons from the universal to the particular, as opposed to materialistic, exoteric science which reasons from the particular to the general—seldom even reaching the universal.

Esotericism involves an effort to live attuned to the inner realities of life. We need to look beyond the quantitative and discover the quality latent within every form. We need to view the apparent meaninglessness of so many events and uncover the meaning behind them. We need to realize that behind every human expression or natural occurrence lies the presence of unconditional love. If we do this our lives will be immensely enriched, led by the attractive power of purpose which animates every cause and every effect.

Esoteric Practice

To help us live esoterically there are several suggestions that can prove beneficial:

a. Make a decision to know yourself more in terms of the qualities you are—that is, discover your uniqueness.

b. Begin a dialogue with your Higher Self, the Soul that you are, to develop discrimination between the personality 'voices' that are limiting and illusory, and that 'still small voice' that is your own inherent wisdom.

c. Conduct a daily review of motives before retiring for the night. Mentally go back over the day (in reverse order, if possible) and acknowledge your motivation in the various things you said or did. Some will have been motivated by selfishness and separatism. *Do not label or judge any thought or action as good or bad.* The point of the exercise is to become conscious of unconscious motives. By becoming conscious, you increase your freedom and power to choose in the future.

d. Keep a journal in which you make a daily notation about any insights you may have experienced during the day. This practice opens the doorway to further insight gained by intuition and allows the Soul more access to the personality.

e. Practice concentration or focusing the mind. Just as the Soul is the link between life and form, so the mind is the link between Soul and personality. The vast majority of humanity cannot control the mind and direct its searchlight for understanding where it wants. Living more in emotions and the past, the individual usually finds the mind to be controlled or conditioned by these. If the mind is to be the vehicle for higher exploration and deeper penetration, we must learn to control it. We can learn to do this by voluntarily directing our attention to what we choose and holding our attention on it for as long as we decide, always returning to the object of focus when the mind wanders. A simple way of practicing this is to keep your mind on what you are doing.

f. Start a routine of daily meditation when you come to the section in this book that discusses the subject.

g. Look for meaningful connections between:
   —Apparently unconnected events
   —Parts and the whole

h. When you experience something ask your Self why you are experiencing it—that is, what is the cause? What is the meaning? What is the purpose? There are many levels of response to all of these questions. Keep asking 'why?' to take you to the limits of your awareness. Do not become overly preoccupied with this exercise as too much questioning will rob you of the enriching possibilities of pure and simple experiencing.

Rhythm

When a person's life is not working very well—when there is excessive stress or unresolved conflict, when things go awry and/or plans are thwarted—it is a sign that rhythm is not present in one's life or in some aspect of it.

Energy—and all is energy—exists in one of three states:

—*Inertia*: is being stuck, lazy, immobile; there is lack of insight, motivation, direction or purpose; it may involve knowing what to do (mental) but not wanting to do it (emotional), or wanting something but not knowing how to attain it, or not having the physical energy or skill to work for it. *Inertia is a state of potentiality.* It is a state of the raw energy of possibilities that can be stimulated to produce certain results.

—*Activity*: is movement of potential; it may be meaningful and purposeful, or lack direction. Ideally all activity—be it physical, emotional or mental—ought to be conscious and therefore purposefully directed toward some desired outcome that is perceived to be beneficial, producing a greater state of integration and harmony. To be meaningful and beneficial, activity must reflect some aspect of Beauty, Truth or Goodness. When it does, it produces a deep sense of satisfaction and fulfillment. When it does not, there still might be some superficial and temporary satisfaction or gratification. Examples of the latter include "getting even" with someone, self-justification, rationalization, blowing off steam and so forth. These activities frequently bring a temporary satisfaction, but leave one feeling empty or out of balance in the long run because the activities do not reflect one's perception of Beauty, Truth or Goodness.

—*Rhythm*: is a personality or form way of being—being in harmony with the purpose of one's True Self, the Soul. It is acting, thinking and feeling which manifests one's higher nature and therefore represents the fact of Unity. It is the revelation, through the personality, of Soul qualities such as love, gratitude, peace, compassion, simplicity, courage and detachment. It is a response to the essential Goodness, the higher Truth, and the latent Beauty present within oneself, within others, and within every potential.

The Soul is a state of *being* and as such is *not* rhythmical; it is integrative or disintegrative. The Soul is either radiating or emanating its energy, itself, to produce integration between itself and its vehicles of expression, or to produce a clearer pathway for its expression by destroying and eliminating obstacles that have been created by inertia, glamors and illusions.

Rhythm is a characteristic of *function*, not being. So when the Soul *functions through* the personality or form it always does so rhythmically. It is the task of the personality, when it becomes conscious of itself as a vehicle of the Soul, to align itself with this rhythmic presence. In so doing it will fulfill a higher purpose and experience a deep and lasting joy that always characterizes the alignment of essence and form, Soul and personality.

Every Soul urge has the ultimate purpose of integrating disparate elements in its vehicles of expression and bringing about a redemption of the parts into the whole, the particulars into the universal and the personal into the impersonal. The *whole*, the *universal* and the *impersonal* are the characteristics of the fifth kingdom—the kingdom of Souls to which we are consciously striving or unconsciously gravitating. It is these three characteristics that elevate incomplete activity and function to a rhythmic state of being in which love, understanding and power are totally present.

What stands in the way of reaching this state of being and maintaining it as a constant source of enlightened functioning is *selfishness*. When we place the little self before the greater Self and look for the short term gain rather than long term fulfillment, then we focus on the *parts*, the *particulars* and the *personal* as being more important than their higher counterparts—the whole, the universal and the impersonal.

Discipline

Selfishness is noted for its lack of discipline. The little self wants immediate gratification; it wants to remain attached to people, objects and situations that give it a sense of power, usefulness or belonging. In order to overcome selfishness discipline must be practiced. Discipline involves:

—*A perception of something greater,* a way of being more whole, a teaching that is liberating, a higher state of being.

—*Willingness to sacrifice* the temporary satisfaction for a permanent gain.

—*Perseverance* to get through the obstacles of inertia and meaningless activity.

—*Detachment* from externals. (One is controlled by the people and things one is attached to. Detachment releases a person for Self-control, and therefore true Power).

—*Motivation* to pursue priorities that have been determined to be worthy of one's best efforts.

—*Courage* to respond to the inner light of wisdom rather than to the desires of the personality.

—*Aspiration* to be a cause rather than an effect.

—*Dedication* to know and follow the universal laws that determine the rhythmic functioning of life on all levels.

While living a disciplined life is an antidote to selfishness, it is simultaneously the primary way to establish rhythm in one's daily life. Through a disciplined orientation, all the details of living, however apparently insignificant, are re-evaluated in light of one's own inner being. That which contradicts the true inner life is eliminated. Integration of the various activities, feelings and thoughts that are not integrated within oneself are brought patiently into a greater harmony, thus reducing inner and outer conflict. Relationships are focused on as important learning opportunities in which to express one's true self. Time and energy are devoted to establishing and maintaining a meaningful inner relationship with one's true Self, gradually allowing the Soul to control the personal life. As the Soul controls the life and all events—which It does automatically when our little selves step out of the way and learn to cooperate with Its integrative and disintegrative emanations—personal rhythm prevails. When the personality functions rhythmically, one is in tune with not only one's own Soul, but the Soul of others and the Soul of the Planetary Life encountered in all relationships and circumstances. A person is then in harmony with all that happens, can sense the purpose of things that happen, can recognize and respond appropriately to need and becomes spontaneously creative. The deeper result of rhythmic living is the attainment of the responsibility, along with the appropriate power, love and knowledge, to function as redeemer of matter. (To "redeem" originally meant 'to pay the ransom to free slaves from captivity.) Having in fact redeemed one's own material constitution one is then capable of assisting others through work, example or simple presence, to do the same. Anyone who is in the presence of a rhythmic, harmonious being, is always affected through resonance.

Rhythm is deeply natural and therefore has a strong effect on others who are sensitive. Its presence evokes a response from within. Whether it is the Soul urge within a person that is prompting a more rhythmic way of life or the presence of a rhythmical person subtly urging the same response, the initial reaction may appear to be anything but harmonious. In fact, the reaction may be antagonistic or strongly resistant. If there are discordant personality traits that stand in the way, the Soul's disintegrating energies may be felt more strongly than its integrating energies! That which blocks rhythm must first be challenged so that it can be brought into full conscious awareness, and then eliminated through the power of consciousness. In the piecemeal elimination of undesirable elements the state of rhythm is born very naturally.

II

UNITY AND DIVERSITY

Underlying all metaphysical awareness is the postulate, *all is one*. Although science is coming closer to the proof of this maxim, the oneness of all life can only be sensed intuitively. The intuition is a level of awareness beyond the mind, a level of 'wholes' to which the mind ascribes diverse parts and divisions. True esoteric knowledge is derived from intuition, enabling the esotericist to reason from the general to the particular, from the whole to the part, from the impersonal to the personal. The orthodox scientist, often more of an occultist[1] than an esotericist, reasons in the opposite direction—from the particular to the general, from the part to the whole.

Another basic postulate is: *the whole is the cause of the part*. This implies that every singular thing or event is part of some greater reality from which it derives its life and existence, the cause of its being and the quality of its nature. The whole of anything is not an absolute, but a relative unity of various elements that constitute its integrity or coherence, identifiable as a whole unit or being. It may, from one's particular vantage point, appear to be an absolute. This unit of wholeness is, in turn, part of a greater whole—ad infinitum—an endless, infinite chain of units forming greater and greater wholes that eventually extend into such a vast unity that human awareness can only stand in awe and wonder. But because of the axiom, "as above, so below" and its corollary, "as below, so above," we assume that since this endless chain of cause and effect, whole and parts, exists without exception within the realms where human awareness can perceive, the process of causation and existence must continue in the same way beyond our awareness.

"All is one" is a way of saying "all is energy." Energy is really not definable, but we can describe it esoterically as being Life itself, distinguishable as both life and consciousness. Although consciousness has many levels such as instinct, subconscious, self-consciousness, group-conscious-

---

[1]See the Introduction for the definition of 'occult.'

ness and God-consciousness, it is in a fundamental sense the ability of a life (be it atomic, mineral, plant, animal, human, planetary, solar, etc.) to relate to another life. Life energy, as part of the one Life, is existence or that which sustains an expression of life in its given state or form.

For example, a plant has both life and consciousness.

—It exists in "its" identifiable form. That is its life.

—It has the ability to relate to other expressions of life such as the sun and the minerals from which it lives. That is its consciousness.

Absolutely everything which we can name or perceive has both life and consciousness, expressions of a greater life and a more inclusive consciousness.

The evolutionary drive inherent within all life is the magnetic energy relationship between effect and cause. The cause is the greater life or larger whole. Cause is intrinsic, not extrinsic to the part. *The cause is within the effect;* the whole is within the part and imbues every aspect of it as a *potential* seeking actualization. This potential is the evolutionary impetus to become the whole.

The direct application of this principle can easily be seen in our own human nature. Our personality is composed of many parts—physical, emotional and mental. When we gain sufficient coordination of the various parts of our physical body, which happens early in our life, we can function as a physical body or physical being. When we activate our emotional nature and can respond to a wide range of stimuli with our feelings we can be emotionally conscious. When we are able to use the many facets of the mind we become mental persons. To be physical, emotional and mental are potentials that are activated through experience of the component parts of each of these units or wholes. Once these units exist as actualities and we are conscious within them, there begins an evolutionary response to the next level of wholeness which is described as 'personality integration'. The three personality components begin to function in a more integrated way, dying to the previous separate way of being and assuming a new life as a unified personality. The consciousness of each part also changes, becoming significantly more inclusive. Greater inclusiveness enhances the capacity to understand more; in this case that means possessing the ability to understand self as personality, other personalities and all component parts of personality. The understanding possessed by an integrated personality is indeed great and such a person is often recognized as a powerful person.

A personality, however, is but a part of a larger whole present within the personality as cause, just as the personality was a cause of the physical, emotional and mental parts. The cause of the personality and its magnetic pull to a greater life is the Soul. As soul-infusion gradually takes place a new life and new consciousness emerge. The personality dies as a separate entity and a shift takes place to an identification with the Soul. The entity now functions within the Soul energy, capable of expressing itself as Soul, and thereby being all that the Soul is.

What we have just seen is an example of the evolution of life and consciousness which has its parallels throughout creation in the seven kingdoms of nature.

Human Parts or Levels	Kingdoms of Nature
1. Physical body	1. mineral
2. Etheric body[1]	2. plant
3. Emotional body	3. animal
4. Mental body	4. human
Integrated personality	higher human[2]
5. Soul	5. Soul
6. Group	6. Planetary
7. Monad	7. Solar

There is an incessant movement of consciousness from 1 through 7 in stepwise progression. The consciousness of each part or each level is both a response to the inherent life of the succeeding whole or level and an expression of it. The *life energy* itself moves in the opposite direction as cause from 7 to 1.

This process of dying as a part and becoming more whole appears to go on endlessly. It is a fundamental process of life. It is described variously as death and rebirth, evolution, initiation, transformation and growth.

To progress in an evolutionary sense, which to the esotericist is an evolution of consciousness rather than of physical life forms, each kingdom of nature goes through a transformation in which it dies to its own kingdom and becomes part of the life and consciousness of the next kingdom in the hierarchical order of life. This means, for example, that the next major step in the evolving consciousness of a human being (4th kingdom) is to become identified with the Soul (5th kingdom). The way

---

[1]Not referred to in our example.

[2]Not a separate kingdom, but the perfection of the fourth kingdom, and therefore developmentally distinct.

of doing this is through the drama of Initiations. In brief, the process involves the following:

— Learning mastery of the physical laws and the ways of matter, and adding to them a dimension of love expressed as *giving*;

— Changing emotional reactiveness into sensitive feeling responses by opening a heartfelt receptivity to *Beauty* which is inherent in all of life's expressions. This stage also involves the learning of emotional detachment so that compassion can be felt and expressed;

— Developing the mind in such a way that it can grasp higher laws, principles and archetypes as embodiments of *truths*, and can formulate these into clear thoughts expressed in rational thinking, in clear words and in meaningful action. Open to truth and less influenced by the conditioning of the past, the mind can then overcome illusion.

It is not enough simply to die[1] at one level to advance to the next to assure attainment of a more inclusive consciousness.

— First, the dying[2] cannot happen until one has brought others up to the same level of consciousness as oneself. These 'others' may include other people, and definitely include the three lower levels (physical, emotional and mental) being brought up to the level of the consciousness of the integrated personality.

— Second, the new level becomes real and truly attained by assuming responsibility for the previous level. From the perspective of the individual this means that the Soul assumes responsibility for the personality. This is why the Soul is called 'The Inner Guide.' From the planetary perspective this means that the spiritual planetary Hierarchy assumes responsibility for Humanity. This is why the Hierarchy is often referred to as 'The Elder Brothers.'[3]

Reality of the Whole

The spiritual language that describes 'all is one' or 'all is energy' is very familiar. The reality is frequently referred to as God, the Divine or Spirit. So we can equally say that all is God, all is Divine, all is Spirit. Just as

---

[1] 'To die' here means 'to leave.'

[2] 'Dying' here means 'to complete.' Completion cannot occur until the whole that one belongs to (a group of fellow humans/the various bodies comprising the personality) is sufficiently unified in one's consciousness.

[3] cf. Chapter XVII—*Questions and Answers.*

there is nothing which is not energy, so there is nothing which is not divine or spiritual or of God.

"Spirituality" is riddled with materialistic attitudes in which all kinds of divisions are made. Cause and effect are seen as separate, and linked extrinsically in time and space. Therefore, it is often thought that there must be a real separation between creator and created, God and man, spirit and matter. The religionist might say that God is in his creation but is separate from it. These separations of cause and effect, whole and part, are products of the lower mind which can only think in such separate ways.

Through *intuition* we are able to perceive the deeper connections and the unity of diverse elements. We can experience that cause is an *intrinsic* energy of every effect, the effect being only a lower level manifestation of its cause. It is not a separate entity, but a partial manifestation of a causal whole. *God* describes a whole and therefore a cause of all that is manifest. Everything manifest is not a plethora of entities separate from God, but God in manifestation. So, too, *spirit* is but a word that describes matter or material reality at a causal level; and *matter* is a relative term that describes spirit at a manifest level of effect. For the sake of convenience we usually draw an arbitrary line between God and creation, spirit and matter where there appears to be a division between formlessness and form. Since there is a vast, overlapping grey area here much confusion can arise. Referring to the previous chart of the Human Parts or Levels the line is usually drawn between the fourth and fifth levels. The overlapping area where both form and formlessness is consciously present is in the integrated personality which corresponds to the higher mind. Sometimes this higher mind is seen as part of the Soul and at times as part of the personality.

So the *mind that is unenlightened* by intuition often says that what is divine and spiritual is exclusively of the fifth, sixth and seventh kingdoms of nature, while that which is of the first four kingdoms is not divine or spiritual. Its conclusions are obvious:

—The human kingdom is not divine, is sinful, bad or wrong in some way.

—The kingdoms below the human are even less worthy, being further removed from divine or spiritual nature, and can therefore be used in any way we choose.

Thus, the inherent divine nature (which gives an entity its value, meaning and purpose) is not recognized or acknowledged and therefore cannot be related to appropriately. Consequently it will be abused.

We often speak of the need for redemption and frequently imply the need to restore the form levels to their higher formless counterparts. While this is true, it is still a narrow view conditioned by materialistic spirituality. It would be more accurate to say that redemption is a process of evolution that occurs when the unconditional love of a more inclusive level of consciousness magnetically draws into itself a lower level of consciousness, thus raising the lower into its higher or truer nature. This occurs *naturally* at all levels—formed or formless. In evolution the higher does not enter the lower, but the lower is drawn into the higher. This is because the higher is more inclusive or 'bigger' and can not be contained in the lower.

The law of correspondences—the hermetic axiom 'as above, so below'—must never be forgotten. The 'above' is God, but as *macrocosm*; the 'below' is God, but as *microcosm*. Are they two separate realities? Certainly not. They are but the larger view and the smaller view of the same reality. They are *views*, not objective realities. As we remember this we can speak of spirit and matter, or soul and personality as apparently different, knowing they are not mutually exclusive, only different levels of the one reality called God, energy, life, or consciousness.

Unity and Trinity

It is unavoidably futile to express the inexpressible—the absolute unity or synthesis of all life and existence—in words. This is why we find such references couched in language that conveys little more than the fact that it is a reality beyond our mind's capability to grasp. We have such descriptions as 'the All,' 'the Whole,' 'the Void,' 'the Unspeakable,' 'the Ineffable One,' 'The One About Whom Naught May Be Said.' To some this is God, but it is not an approachable Being since it is beyond conscious relationship. Any 'God' that Man approaches through prayer, supplication or invocation must be one that Man can experience consciously, albeit at the outer limits of awareness. For the average human being this 'God' is the individual Soul experienced primarily as love; for the more conscious human being this 'God' is the planetary Soul called the Hierarchy or Kingdom of Souls who embody the Plan of Love of the Planetary Life or Kingdom. To the Soul-infused personality functioning consciously within the Planetary Life, the Solar Being becomes the 'God' of contact. This Solar Being is initially known in its primary aspect of Love. There are greater 'Gods' or levels of Oneness beyond the Solar system, but Man *in* this system has his consciousness restricted *to* this system to derive maximum benefit from the life within the system.

From the unknowable Void where nothing (no thing) exists, beyond time and space, in that realm which we call infinity, there emerges the principle of life without time, space and form. This principle is symbolized by the number *1*. It suggests a *source* rather than a beginning. *Source* is a reference point from which something flows while *beginning* suggests a point before which there is no existence. The *1* is sometimes called 'the dimensionless point', *no thing* (•). When extended the point becomes a line segment with two end points (•—•); when *1* expresses itself it sets up a possible *duality*—the expressor and the expression, hence potential relationship or *2*. When *1* and *2* interact a third reality comes into being, symbolically forming a triangle which is a *completed form of energy* (Δ).

The triangle effectively represents the three basic principles of any whole or natural unity and of any and all levels. These three principles are the knowable emanations of the unknowable ALL. They are the three Universal Laws that constitute all existence: the *Law of Synthesis*, the *Law of Attraction* and the *Law of Economy*. They are the *purpose*, the *meaning* and the *activity* of life and consciousness. They are the *spirit*, the *soul* and the *form* of every reality. They are inherent in every creation, in every potential and in all evolving realities. They exist in the macrocosm and the microcosm at all levels. We can chart some of the correspondences of the 'divine trinity' in the following way:

THREE ASPECTS OF ENERGY/DIVINITY

First	Second	Third
Synthesis	Attraction	Economy
Spirit	Consciousness	Matter
Life	Consciousness	Form
Purpose	Plan/Meaning	Activity
Power	Love	Light
Father	Child	Mother
Spirit/Monad	Soul	Personality
Mental	Astral	Etheric-Physical
Mind	Emotion	Physical body
Shamballa	Hierarchy	Humanity
Will	Being	Function
Being	Quality	Quantity
Male	Androgyny	Female
Father	Son	Holy Spirit
Existence	Essence	Substance

When something (including a human being) comes into existence, the source of that existence is the first aspect; it is here that we can say the process begins because it is here that we find the life energy itself. By definition, the first aspect is purposeful. Because everything begins here, everything has a purpose. In the emanation of itself it seeks the third aspect with which to relate and in which to implant its life energy, giving rise to an activation or movement.

The third aspect is an opposite to the first aspect and because of opposition it is receptive to it and attractive to it.

The interplay of these two aspects automatically produces the second aspect, the middle or mediating point, the dynamic point of tension and cohesion where consciousness arises.

Consciousness is a product of the presence of opposites. When, for example, we are faced with two opposing forces such as conflicting desires, and we have to choose between them we go through a process of becoming more aware of the pros and cons of each alternative so that we can make a wiser or more conscious choice. When opposites interact consciousness is produced; it then becomes a first aspect.[1] As such it seeks further interaction with a corresponding third aspect, the result of which will be the creating of more consciousness. On and on it goes in an ever ascending spiral towards a reunification of life, consciousness and form.

Because the three aspects of divinity or principles of energy are always present simultaneously, and only separable by abstraction, we know that every act, event and circumstance has meaning and purpose. If an individual or a society does not have a sense of meaning and purpose it will be either excessively materialistic or controlled by the superficial third aspect (personality, matter, quantity, events, circumstances). Force, manipulation and egotism consequently tend to prevail. In this case, altruism, service and unconditional love mean nothing. Caught in a meaningless and purposeless existence, one is faced with futility, suffering and even desperation. This plight often takes one to the brink of despair where the Light of consciousness can begin to dawn. But even if despair is avoided, suffering alone can often lead one to the awakening of consciousness. That, in fact, is the purpose of suffering. All suffering is but the interaction of the first and third aspects which has not as yet produced the second aspect—consciousness. What blocks the final outcome of awakening is an excessive preoccupation or identification with either the

---

[1]Consciousness, by its very nature, is creative and initiatory. It naturally assume a 'first aspect' role as it expresses these qualities.

first or third aspects. For example, if you are excessively mentally polarized or inordinately focused on physical gratification, it is difficult to *feel* what you need or to feel what others are experiencing. You will therefore probably suffer great lack of personal fulfillment as well as suffer difficulty in relationships. This suffering will become sufficiently unbearable that you will let go of some of your mentalization or physical preoccupation and allow yourself to feel more. Such a time in one's life is usually a *crisis*, but it is meaningful and purposeful. The Chinese ideogram for crisis is 'danger' and 'opportunity'. Everyone attempts to avoid crises because these feel dangerous to our security and well-being; but the stirring of life to produce consciousness is definitely an opportunity to enlarge oneself and become more whole. However the part, the little ego, that is created by the past wants to remain in the past which it knows and where it is comfortable. A new awareness is a movement to the unknown, and adjustments in living are required to find a new way of being comfortable. This tendency of the ego toward fixation, comfort and the known is nature's way of making sure that the new conscious awareness always becomes integrated with the old and the past, thus grounding it and allowing the new to 'fertilize' and affect the old to begin its transformation.

The esotericist is open to new possibilities for change and expression so that the inner energies can be outwardly expressed, so the life can be conscious and every new consciousness attained can be a vehicle for giving life in service. Remember that consciousness *is* love and it is love which is the energy of service allowing others to touch the love within themselves and thereby growing in awareness.

The esotericist looks for meaning and purpose as the revealers of Beauty, Truth and Goodness. The power and inspiration they provide facilitate every decision and enable one to flow with life in a more inclusive, less selfish way.

Trinity in Multiplicity

It is traditionally taught that the One Life of the Supreme Being manifests in the Universe as a trinity. From this trinity, through all possible combinations, a septenary is formed. The septenary includes the original trinity and is the totality of all that exists in manifest life.

We speak of seven *planes of existence*:

1. The Divine, The ALL, The Logoic
2. The Monadic
3. The Atmic

  4. The Buddhic/Intuitive
  5. The Mental—Higher (abstract)
             —Lower (concrete)
  6. The Astral
  7. The Etheric-Physical

The act of creation proceeds from 1 through 7, with each preceding plane creating or manifesting the subsequent plane. However, from another perspective we can say that the first three create the remaining four. There is also a special relationship of resonance between alternate planes. Planes 1, 3, 5 and 7 affect each other in a unique way, as do 2, 4 and 6. These planes are often referred to as dimensions and are considered to be divisible into seven sub-planes. An example of this can be seen in the etheric-physical dimension:

  1. First etheric: atomic
  2. Second etheric: subatomic
  3. Third etheric: super etheric
  4. Fourth etheric: etheric/ionic
  5. Gaseous
  6. Liquid
  7. Solid

The manifestation of life and creativity proceeds 'downward', according to our charts, the whole manifesting in ever greater diversity, complexity and partiality. The development of consciousness, on the other hand, proceeds 'upward.' As each lower level or part is experienced and mastered, consciousness 'expands' to include a greater whole. This progressive ascent into inclusiveness and simplicity is referred to as 'the Path of Return,' 'the Way Home,' or 'the return of the prodigal son to the Father's House.'

The septenary system is found throughout life and is in our every attempt to describe whole systems. An example of this is the Seven Kingdoms of Nature found within our Solar System. These are but seven levels of consciousness of the Solar Being:

  1. Solar Kingdom
  2. Planetary Kingdom
  3. Soul Kingdom
  4. Human Kingdom
  5. Animal Kingdom
  6. Plant Kingdom
  7. Mineral Kingdom

III

THE SEVEN RAYS

Origin and Facts

The septenary nature of life is often now referred to as seven *rays*, but in times past was referred to by such phrases as 'Seven Spirits before the throne' or such images as the 'Seven Rishis of the Great Bear' and the 'Seven Sisters of the Pleiades.'

Every universe, galaxy, sun, solar system and planet is but the physical life of a Great Being in much the same way as our bodies are but the physical lives of lesser beings called human beings.

The *Seven Spirits* refer to the seven sacred planets—Vulcan, Jupiter, Saturn, Mercury, Venus, Neptune and Uranus. The *Seven Rishis* are considered the seven head centers in the body of the 'One About Whom Naught Be Said.' The *Seven Sisters* are said to be the throat center of the same Great Being.

The seven rays are traced to the Great Bear as the origin of the septenary division. These rays may be traced even further to their source in the One Life from which they emanate. The fundamental nature of this singular source is that of *Purpose*—the purpose or divine Will of Life. As the differentiation occurs we discover that all creation can return to the Creator by seven different ways or pathways to fulfill the divine purpose. This differentiation also shows that there is a need to experience all seven ways or rays completely to fulfill the whole Purpose of the Creator.

Each ray is a particular quality permeating the nature of the Creator. Since all else is contained within Him, these ray-qualities are seen as the builders of all the lesser entities that comprise His nature. Not only do they build and maintain the whole Life within all its parts, but they also reside in the parts as divine qualities seeking full expression so that the latent purpose of God can be revealed and His Life fully expressed, thus bringing about the Kingdom of Heaven on earth.

We might note here that the Great Being known as the Solar Logos, embodied in our Sun, is a channel for the second of these seven rays,

31

namely Love-Wisdom. It is because of this we say "God is Love." Other suns within the Milky Way Galaxy are vehicles for other rays. Each of the seven sacred planets represent, as channels, each of the seven rays. Consider the following possibility:

Ray 1—Vulcan
Ray 2—Jupiter
Ray 3—Saturn
Ray 4—Mercury
Ray 5—Venus
Ray 6—Neptune
Ray 7—Uranus

These planets are part of a *second ray solar system* and are representative of the *seven-ray subdivisions of Ray 2*. Just as each color in the spectrum contains all colors, so each single ray contains all rays.

Although the Solar Logos is a channel of Ray 2 energy, it is in fact a trinity as is every being. The God of our Solar system is referred to in its Trinitarian nature as Father, Son and Holy Spirit. In ray terms this translates as Will, Love-Wisdom and Active Intelligence or Light. These are the three primary aspects of Divine Life found anywhere and are called the *three rays of aspect*. When these three are combined, as in the following chart, the *four rays of attribute* are formed.

Ray Combination	Ray Produced	
1 (uncombined)	1	Rays
2 (uncombined)	2	of
3 (uncombined)	3	Aspect
1 and 2	4	Rays
1 and 3	5	of
2 and 3	6	Attribute
1 and 2 and 3	7	

These are all of the possible combinations of the basic trinity. Therefore all that exists is essentially the Divine Trinity: Will or Purpose, Love-Wisdom or Plan, and Active Intelligence or Light. The septenary thus formed represents the full spectrum of consciousness possible for any being. It is through many experiences in many life cycles that the fullness of consciousness is attained. With the varied dynamic relationships between rays governing various aspects of life every being evolves into greater awareness of the One Life in Whom it lives and moves and has its being. The names of the rays vary somewhat as the words used are but attempts to describe the quality of each. When referring to them we usually use only their numerical designation—Ray 1, Ray 2, Ray 3, etc.

Ray	Quality	Field Of Human Activity
1	Will or Power	Politics, government
2	Love-Wisdom	Education, psychology
3	Active Intelligence or Higher Mind	Philosophy, communication
4	Harmony Through Conflict or Beauty	Arts, architecture
5	Lower, Concrete Mind or Knowledge	Science, esoteric psychology
6	Idealism or Devotion	Religion, worship
7	Ceremonial Order or Magic	Finance, organization, economics

We now look at some of the ray characteristics as expressed primarily in the human kingdom. Try to get a feeling or a picture of what each ray represents as a whole, and how it is distinct from all the others.

RAY 1

Strengths:

- Strength (often strength of will)
- One-pointedness
- Strong sense of purpose
- Steadfastness
- The power to detach
- Lawgiver with wisdom
- Law enforcer with gentleness
- Power to rule and govern, including oneself
- Capacity to grasp principles
- Power to lead
- Power to preserve values
- Ability to sense and give purpose

- Independence
- Courage
- Dynamic power
- Power to synthesize
- Fearlessness
- Power to liberate
- Broadmindedness
- Ability to destroy in a beneficial way

- Power to direct
- Power to centralize and organize
- Power to initiate

Weaknesses:

- Pride
- Cruelty
- Violence
- Arrogance
- Control
- Suppression
- Hardness
- Willfulness
- Stubbornness
- Harmful or meaningless destructiveness

- Anger
- Egotism
- Ambition
- Obstinacy
- Oppressiveness
- Inhibition
- Domination over others
- Impatience
- Manipulation

RAY 2

Strengths:

- Calmness
- Magnetic love
- Understanding through love
- Endurance
- Faithfulness
- Empathy
- Refined sensitivity
- Impressionability
- Receptivity
- Inclusiveness
- Tact
- Insight
- Healing power of love
- Spiritual sense
- Loving wisdom
- Attractive love
- Patience
- Love of truth
- Sympathy
- Compassion
- Intuition
- Serene temper
- Clear intelligence
- Power to teach
- Diplomacy
- Tolerance
- Love of study
- Wise counselor
- Desire for absolute truth and pure knowledge

Weaknesses:

- Indifference to others
- Indifference
- Over-attachment
- Lack of energy or lethargy
- Intolerance of mental limitation in others
- Over-inclusiveness
- Tendency toward inferiority complex
- Over-sensitivity
- Coldness
- Fearfulness
- Over-protectiveness
- Excessive absorption in study
- Wanting to be liked and to be popular
- Non-assertiveness
- Self-pity
- Insensitivity

RAY 3

Strengths:

- Active and clear intellect
- Broad understanding of abstract issues

- Capacity for rigorous analysis and reasoning
- Understanding of relativity
- Sincerity of purpose
- Caution
- Adaptability
- Ability to handle money
- Simplification of complexity
- Capacity to theorize
- Capacity for abstract thinking
- Power to manipulate in a positive way to gain results
- Facility with language; using the right and appropriate words
- Mental creativity
- Mental accuracy
- Patience
- Ability to plan
- Economic understanding
- Aptitude for business

Weaknesses:

- Intellectual Pride
- Over-adaptation
- Hyperactivity or excessive busyness
- Absentmindedness
- Obstinacy
- Impractical ideas
- Absence of practical action
- Opportunism
- Amoral materialism
- Scattering of energies
- Manipulation
- Criticism
- Inaccuracy in details
- Isolation
- Intellectualism
- Confusion
- Carelessness
- Deceitfulness
- Disorder
- Excessive preoccupation

RAY 4

Strengths:

- Strong affections
- Love of beauty
- Sense of drama
- Imagination
- Humor
- Harmony and serenity through struggle and crisis
- Sympathy
- Quickness of intellect and perception
- Spontaneity
- Artistry
- Sense of color and beauty
- Creative ability
- Intuition
- Compromising and mediating
- Ability to bring harmony out of conflict
- Generosity
- Devotion
- Peace making ability

Weaknesses:

- Worry
- Constant conflict, struggle, turmoil
- Lack of confidence
- Excessive moodiness
- Strong passions
- Extravagance
- Procrastination
- Temperamental nature
- Exaggeration
- Over-eagerness for compromise
- Self-pity
- Agitation
- Lack of composure
- Lack of moral courage
- Laziness
- Moral cowardice
- Instability and spasmodic action
- Impracticality
- Confusion
- Manic-depressive tendencies

RAY 5

Strengths:

- Accuracy
- Analytical mind
- Keen intellect
- Strictly accurate statements
- Common sense
- Specialization
- Precision
- Detached observation
- Truthfulness
- Perseverance

- Independence
- Ability to think and act scientifically
- Mastery of factual detail
- Mechanical and technical ability
- Reason based on observation
- Perception of cause & effect relationships

- Justice, often without mercy
- Mathematical ability
- Discrimination
- Ability to investigate and research
- Practical inventiveness

Weaknesses:

- Excessive intellectualization
- Lack of sympathy
- Harsh criticism
- Excessive linearity
- Irreverence
- Excessive objectivity
- Set opinions
- Social awkwardness
- Pedantic nature

- Narrowness
- Prejudice
- Over analysis
- Doubt and skepticism
- Lack of intuitive sensitivity
- Rigid thinking
- Lack of emotion
- Intellectual pride

RAY 6

Strengths:

- Devotion
- Love
- Loyalty
- Intuition
- Aspiration
- Visionary
- Religious instincts
- Self sacrifice
- Optimism
- Humility
- Power to arouse, inspire, persuade

- Single-mindedness
- Tenderness
- Reverence
- Idealism
- Mysticism
- Dedication
- Intense personal feeling
- Ardent faith
- Sincerity
- Openness to spiritual guidance
- Persistence

Weaknesses:

- Fanaticism
- Blind follower
- Over dependency on others
- Partiality
- Superstition
- Fiery anger
- Militarism
- Gullibility
- Hypersensitivity
- Unreasoning devotion
- Unnatural suppression of the
  instinctual nature

- Bigotry
- Martyr complex
- Narrow-mindedness
- Selfish and jealous love
- Self-deception
- Prejudice
- Emotionalism
- Blind faith
- Idealistic impracticality
- Extremism
- Excess

- Exclusive devotion to an exclusive God
- Imbalance: seeing things as either perfect or intolerable

RAY 7

Strengths:

- Strength
- Self reliance
- Organization
- Skill in business
- Practicality
- Rhythmic work
- Synthesizing ability
- Adherence to rule and precedence
- Ability to work with the devas
- Power to bring spirit and matter together
- Power to build, renovate, transform
- Power to implement the law
- Courage
- Courtesy
- Order
- Group work
- Ability to manifest ideas
- Ritual
- Decent and ordered conduct
- Magical power
- Power to manifest and to work upon the material plane

Weaknesses:

- Formalism
- Superstition
- Pride
- Superficial judgments
- Rigid orderliness
- Meaningless ritualism
- Intolerance of differences
- Form orientation
- Addiction to phenomena—occult, psychic or otherwise
- Manipulation
- Sex magic
- Narrowness
- Materialistic attitudes
- Bigotry
- Crystallizations
- Rigid routinization
- Lack of originality
- Excessive perfectionism
- Excessive concern with rules, regulations & the letter of the law

With sufficient experience through suffering, through trying to make life work and trying to express oneself, one eventually develops the strengths of the rays. The weaknesses are present by default rather than by design. When the positive quality is lacking, the negative manifests. To reduce the impact of the negative we must emphasize and focus on the positive. Strengths and weaknesses are *dual* aspects of the *same* energy.

Often synthesizing the positive and negative responses to the pure energy of the ray requires drawing upon the energy of a different ray. For example, the arrogance of Ray 1 may need to be tempered by the empathy, sympathy and compassion of Ray 2. Or the narrow-mindedness of the fifth ray may need to be balanced by the wider vision of the third ray.

A knowledge of the rays themselves is a relatively simple matter of learning their respective characteristics. The application of this knowledge is quite another matter, demanding analysis and frequently intuition. There have been several books written about the rays that can prove helpful to the sincere student.[1]

The rays that are useful to consider in connection with humanity and one's own dynamic place within the body of humanity are the following:

1. The ray of the solar system: 2 (personality and soul).
2. The ray of the planetary Logos: 3 (personality ray).
3. The ray of the human kingdom: 4 (soul ray) and 5 (personality ray).
4. The ray of the present root race, the Aryan: 5 (dominant) and 3.
5. The ray of the current cycle, the astrological age: 7 (Aquarian age).[2]
6. The ray of one's own country.[3]
7. The ray of the individual Soul.
8. The ray of the individual personality.
9. The rays governing the individual's:
   —Mental body.
   —Emotional or Astral body.
   —Physical body.

Other ray influences which might prove helpful to know:

The 5th Kingdom (Hierarchy)

   —Ray 5 (working through personality)
   —Ray 2 (working through intuition)

The Path of Discipleship

   —Ray 2, which transmutes knowledge into wisdom and feeds the Christ life and principle in each individual.

---

[1]The first to be written which form the basis for all others subsequently published are *Esoteric Psychology*, Vol. I and II by Alice A. Bailey. The most comprehensive and detailed books published on the application of the rays to human nature are a two-volume series by Michael D. Robbins—*Tapestry of the Gods, Volume I—The Seven Rays: An Esoteric Key To Understanding Human Nature*, and *Volume II—Psycho-spiritual Transformation and The Seven Rays*. An excellent, short treatment of the subject, in which the word 'ray' is never mentioned, is *Psychosynthesis Typology* by Roberto Assiagioli.

[2]The outgoing Piscean age has been governed by Ray 6. Rays 6 and 7 are currently approximately equal in potency and influence.

[3]See the chart, *Rays of Nations*, later in this chapter.

The Path of Initiation

—Ray 1, which produces detachment from form, the destruction of hindrances, and a dynamic will which will enable the initiate to persevere and take the needed steps towards the Initiator.

Self-Assessment

While all of these specific attributions of rays to such realities as the human kingdom, the present cycle, the planetary life, etc. are interesting and helpful, they merely provide the contexts in which the individual functions. As contexts they do influence a person, but the immediate dynamics can only be seen when the individual's rays are determined—the Soul, personality and body rays. The greatest influence on the person is the Soul ray, while the others are subsidiary to it. The Soul ray holds the purpose of the incarnation and is the quality that seeks expression through the vehicles of the personality and threefold lower nature.

Through knowing ourselves at each level of our expression and being we can determine which ray is governing that level. The difficulty is that few people know themselves sufficiently to be able to apply the knowledge of the rays to each of their bodies or Soul. Do you know, for example, the nature of your own mind and the particular way your emotional body functions? And do you know when you are acting from your Soul-centered consciousness as opposed to your personality consciousness? If you cannot distinguish between the various levels, the precise correspondence of level to ray cannot be made. We can, however, come more easily to an approximation of which ray or combination of rays is more dominant in us. This is helpful and a place to start because it will reveal strengths that we can use and weaknesses that need to be overcome. Working with the knowledge we have will lead us into greater knowledge of who we are and how we are. Eventually everyone will experience all the rays and all the possible combinations, so to begin anywhere will serve that end. In fact, on the Path of Initiation, when one is becoming Soul conscious there is experience of all seven rays, and in each lifetime there is a re-enactment of identification with all the rays, although some of that experience will be more symbolic than actual.

There are people dedicated to developing the ray awareness aspects of esoteric psychology and are preparing questionnaires to help people identify their own ray structures. These are proving useful, but nothing is a substitute for self-knowledge. Their value will be gauged by their ability to enhance this self-knowledge.

The following hints may assist you in seeing yourself more clearly in light of the rays.

1. The most common physical body rays are 1, 3, and 7. The next most frequently found are 2 and 6. The least common physical bodies are 4 and 5.

2. The astral (emotional) body is usually Ray 2, 4 or 6.

3. The mental body can really be any ray, but those most often found today are 1, 3, 5 and 7.

4. A third ray mental body is often accompanied by a first ray Soul.

5. Second ray Souls rarely have a third ray mental body.

6. At this time in history there are few fourth ray Souls and fewer first ray Souls in incarnation. Seventh ray Souls were also a rarity but they are increasingly incarnating because of the opportunities emerging within the seventh ray influence of the Aquarian age.

7. Most people on a spiritual path are second ray Souls, although sixth ray Souls are also quite common, especially when the spiritual path is a religious one.

8. The Soul ray changes infrequently, maintaining the same ray for several incarnations and never changing its ray within a lifetime.

9. The Soul changes to one of the three major rays (1, 2 or 3) during discipleship.

10. Knowing one's basic tendencies may give a clue to ray influence:

    Ray 1 and 7   – prone to pride
    Ray 2 and 6   – prone to anger
    Ray 3 and 5   – prone to fear
    Ray 4   – prone to conflict

11. Looking at one's failures and basic weaknesses gives good indications of specific ray influences.

12. Objectively looking at what one's influence on others has been can also be revealing. We tend to relate to others from a certain focus or polarization, such as:

    —when teaching we might be more Soul centered.

    —when relating to our family we might be emphatically more emotional.

    —when dealing with business we may tend to be mentally focused.

The characteristics which are present in each of those situations will suggest which ray is being expressed through the particular body or level of consciousness prevailing.

13. Since the Soul urge is one's deepest desire or aspiration we can ask ourselves what we most want in life after we put aside our wishes and desires. The answer may reveal the Soul ray. We might use the following list as a guide:

Ray	Principle, Ideal, Quality	Guiding Light	Power
1	Freedom	Courage	Will
2	Unity	Love	Love
3	Understanding	Truth	Thought (Light)
4	Harmony	Courage	Imagination
5	Truth	Truth	Thought (Light)
6	Goodness	Love	Love
7	Beauty	Courage	Will

It can be noted here that the first three rays are outwardly reflected in the last three: 1 reflected in 7, 2 in 6 and 3 in 5. This is the reason there is much similarity between these pairs.

A sustained question over a period of time will bring the insight sought. This question might be stated: "In times of deepest need or crisis do I rely mostly on mind and thought (ray 3 & 5), love (ray 2 or 6) or power and will (1 or 7), to bring about a satisfactory resolution of the problem?" The answer points to the Soul ray because it is the Soul who rescues the personality in time of greatest crisis. That sustained question may be more simply stated as "What is my Soul ray?" Let the answer come to your mind from the Soul in whatever way it can.

There is such a vast amount of information and knowledge about the rays that it is difficult to put in few words that which is essential. Perhaps the following notes will be helpful in rounding out this brief presentation.

The Rays—Miscellaneous Notes

1. Ray 4 is one of the most difficult rays to understand clearly. It deals with issues of conflict, and conflict is present throughout humanity. Humanity, governed by ray 4, has the unique purpose of standing in the middle of all seven kingdoms. Its task, therefore, is to function as a middle principle or the mediating point between the higher and the lower. Ray 4 has the same purpose of being the mediating point between Rays 5, 6 and 7 and 1, 2 and 3. The fourth (ray or kingdom) is where the outer and the inner come together to be harmonized. It is a place where conflict exists and crisis is present. It is precisely at this point, whether in the kingdoms or in the rays, that the principle of Soul creation exists. Souls are born out of conflict—of the ultimate conflict between spirit and matter seen as in opposition.

When Spirit's life is first felt in matter, the fire of this life burns in a destructive way to release life from *inertia*. Then as the presence intensifies it leads to *chaos* (activity) with no perception of wrong or right. This then develops into *conflict* when the opposites are perceived or developed through the activity that emerges. It is working with this duality that leads one to look for resolution. When resolution is attained Soul consciousness emerges. Duality serves the purpose of revealing all sides of a reality and in the process the quality is perceived beyond the form or inherent within the form behind the quantity or matter aspect. Within the quality there is a balancing of the opposites; rhythm emerges from the polar swings. Thus the Soul or essence of the reality is contacted. Conflict and chaos, and the accompanying indecision, exist in order to stimulate the astral body and the emotions into awakening desire. Initially this desire is for pleasurable harmony. Until desire is awakened the Soul or quality will not be sought after. This basic desire for pleasurable harmony is a reflection of the highest state of pure harmony or being, the state of our destiny. Desire is but a lower reflection of the higher reality which is Divine Will. When this desire emerges, quality is not sought for its own sake, or because it is a true Self, or a reflection of Divine Will, but because it makes life more pleasurable, more desirable and easier.

The principle of conflict is absolutely necessary in the human kingdom so we may learn to choose and to make *decisions*. The word 'decision' means 'to die into God.' Our ultimate purpose is to die to the lower in order to be reborn into the higher, into the fullness of energy or Godness. At pre-conflict stages, the person is controlled by physical tendencies (pain-pleasure), conditioning and selfish desires. The conflict must become severe enough so the person is forced to develop will and use that will for good, for controlling rather than being controlled. Eventually, through the decision-making process, the level of control shifts slowly higher over the ensuing evolution.

The three powers or levels characteristic of the fourth kingdom, Man's, are instinct, intellect and intuition. Man's instinct is derived from his animal nature or the animal kingdom (Ray 3), while intellect is the product of Ray 5 peculiar to the human kingdom and the intuition is a product from Ray 4, also peculiar to the human kingdom. From this attribution of intuition to fourth ray influence we can see how essential the fourth ray is to higher human development where animal man becomes a Soul being.

2. Rays of Nations[1]

Nation	Soul Ray	Personality Ray
Africa	6	7
Albania	2	7
Argentina	1	6
Australia	2	7
Austria	4	5
Belgium	5	7
Brazil	4	2
Bulgaria	6	7
Canada	2	1
China	1	3
Czechoslovakia	4	6
Denmark	3	2
Egypt	1	7
Europe	4	3
Finland	3	2
France	5	3
Germany	4	1
Great Britain	2	1
Greece	1	3
Holland	5	7
Hungary	6	4
Iceland	3	4
India	1	4
Indonesia	6	2
Ireland	6	6
Italy	6	4
Japan	6	4
Jugoslavia	6	7
Norway	2	4
Poland	6	6
Portugal	6	7
Romania	6	7
Russia	7	6
Spain	6	7
Sweden	3	2
Switzerland	2	3
Turkey	3	6
U.S.A.	2	6

[1]Some of these are found in *A Treatise On The Seven Rays* by A.A. Bailey. Some are given by Benjamin Creme in publications of Share International.

3. Meditation/Work. There are some suggested ways of achieving the incorporation of each of the rays in our human response to their energies. This can be done through meditation, through effort and work.

Ray	Meditation/Work
1	Initiation
2	Vision
3	Education
4	Intuition
5	Liberation
6	Idealism
7	Organization

4. The Planets and the Rays. There is an interesting and potentially revealing association between the rays and the planets.

Ray	Sacred Planet
1	Vulcan
2	Jupiter
3	Saturn
4	Mercury
5	Venus
6	Neptune
7	Uranus

Ray	Non-Sacred Planet
1	Pluto
2	Sun (veiling a hidden planet)
3	Earth
4	Moon (veiling a hidden planet)
6	Mars

Certain sacred planets and certain non-sacred planets have a close relation with each other and the rays that influence them.[1] These are:

Ray 1—Vulcan, Pluto
Ray 2—Jupiter, Sun
Ray 3—Saturn, Earth
Ray 4—Mercury, Moon
Ray 6—Neptune, Mars

---

[1] cf. Bailey, A.A., *Esoteric Psychology*, Vol, I. 335-338. (All references to A.A. Bailey are published by Lucis Trust. These extracts may not be reprinted except by permission from Lucis Trust which holds copyright.)

5. The Souls of all human beings can be found to be on any of the seven rays.

6. After the stage of Soul/personality integration referred to as the *Third Initiation;* all Souls are on one of the three major rays.

7. The ray of the Monad of every person is one of the three rays of aspect so that we are either Monads of power, of love, or of intelligence.

8. There comes a point in every person's development when the personality ray becomes dominant and the three bodies are subordinated to it. Then a great struggle takes place and a tension is set up between the Soul ray and the personality ray. The sense of duality becomes definitely established. This crisis is reflected in the Bhagavad Gita where the experiences of the path of discipleship are described. Arjuna stands at the midpoint on the field of Kurukshetra, between the two opposing forces. The struggle he faces, which is the struggle of the Soul, is described as a battle, for that it truly is.

9. When each individual aspirant arrives at an understanding of his Soul ray, personality ray, his mental, emotional and physical ray then he will indeed have fulfilled the injunction: "know thyself," and can therefore take initiation. It is far better not to have someone else who supposedly may know or have intuitive ability to tell you what your rays are. It is far better to go through the more lengthy, but enriching experience, to discover your own rays. Only in this way will you truly get to know yourself.

10. We always find correspondences or resonances between higher and lower. We therefore can see the following influences: the personality ray, which is always difficult to determine, expresses through the physical body and the physical plane. We can see it manifest through a person's appearance and occupation, life trends and purpose. The Soul ray tends to show its influence on the astral body, causing a struggle in one's emotional life as it works at transforming glamors. The Monadic ray has its stronger influence on the mental body once the integration of the personality has taken place. Here it works to overcome illusion and produce clear vision.

11. In the three aspects of divinity or existence—i.e., life (will), quality (love) and appearance (light) we note:

—the *appearance* aspect exists as duality;

—the *quality* aspect exists as duality up to the Third Initiation (e.g., the lover and the loved, the desirer and the desired, the seeker and the sought);

—the *life* aspect exists beyond duality, and is not apprehended until beyond the Third Initiation.

Duality is the work of the mind, as is division. Hence, also the seven rays are a product of the mind's tendency to separate reality into its component parts. In this way, through experience of the parts, the whole can eventually be consciously embraced and entered with full power, love and light.

12. There is a relationship between the rays and the centers within the body. Not all sources agree which ray governs which center. Following are the associations given in *Esoteric Psychology* by Alice Bailey.

Ray	The Center
1	Head (Crown)
2	Heart
3	Throat
4	Base of Spine
5	Brow
6	Solar plexus
7	Sacral

13. It is interesting to note the ray influences in the various kingdoms and the power or energy resulting from those ray influences which are characteristic of each kingdom.

Kingdom	Ray	Energy Characteristics
Mineral	7	Radiation or Radioactivity.
	1	The basic reservoir of power.
Vegetable	2	Magnetism.
	4	Uniformity and harmony of color.
	6	Upward tendency or growth toward light.
Animal	3	Instinct.
	6	Domesticity.
Human	5	Intellect.
	4	Experience, growth leading to intuition.
Souls	5	Personality.
	2	Intuition.
Planetary	6	The Plan.
	3	Creative Work.
Solar	1	Universal Mind, Will.
	7	Synthetic ritual.

14. One of the practical ways of using our knowledge of the seven rays is to incorporate them into our writing, our teaching and our communica-

tion with others. Everyone is governed by different rays, so if we can learn to encompass the qualities of all of the rays in our relationships we then become universal and able to relate to all people. We also, in this way, go through the seven steps of wholeness or completeness whether that be in a lecture, a class, a composition or a way of approaching. Everybody has their own particular learning styles and communication styles. These are determined by a person's ray constitution. The following are the various elements to be included into a whole, listed according to the sequence of the rays.

Ray 1—showing purpose; promoting self reliance; awakening.

Ray 2—presenting an overview; giving the meaning and quality; using examples; group sharing.

Ray 3—presenting a variety of ideas from different points of view; analysis; group discussion.

Ray 4—providing something experiential, evoking intuition and feeling; using examples; humor; creative images; presenting beauty, harmony and balance which inspire.

Ray 5—being logical and rational; giving details; being accurate; demonstrating practical application.

Ray 6—strong presentation of ideals about which one can feel very good or inspired and with which one can identify; emphasizing values.

Ray 7—doing something (learning by doing); efficiency; being organized; tying everything together; sequential (cause and effect); using repetition.

15. We are living in a time of significant change and transition, a time of crisis. We are moving from one astrological age to another, from the Piscean to the Aquarian age. This transition is indicated by a change of ray influence—the important context of the cycles that influence humanity. The Piscean age was characterized by Ray 6; the Aquarian age is characterized by Ray 7. There is a unique relationship between the Piscean and Aquarian age in terms of the rays as there is a unique relationship between the sixth ray and the seventh ray. It apparently is somewhat unusual that two sequential rays follow each other in terms of cyclic influence. The sixth ray and Piscean age has had the purpose of preparing humanity for the significant changes that are to occur during the seventh ray Aquarian age. Let us contrast the two briefly and show their relationships.

Sixth Ray (Piscean age)	Seventh Ray (Aquarian age)
Fostering ideals and visions.	Applying the ideals and visions in practical reality, thereby producing magic.
Development of the mystic.	Development of the magician.
Separatism—such as nationalism and sectarianism	Unity, fusion and synthesis—such as internationalism.
Groups of disciples were formed but not interacting, often based on personality reactions.	Groups of initiates are formed working in unison with each other and with the Plan.
Duality was emphasized, reflected in the attitude of the academic, materialistic psychologists.	A sense of higher unity is inaugurated, working toward personality integration for the masses and of Soul-body fusion for aspirants and disciples.
Education emphasized development of the intellect.	Education which emphasizes development of intuition.
The meaning of sacrifice was taught. Philanthropy on one level and "being kind" on another level were expressions of the inauguration of service.	The consciousness of the coming initiates will embrace the concept of group service and group sacrifice inaugurating the age of "divine service". Personal sacrifice will be made to serve as a group by those more advanced, and kinship will be the keynote for the rest of humanity.
Growth of the spirit of individuals and the development of individual consciousness.	The development of group consciousness and group spirit.
The historical Christ was recognized and the teaching of love was begun.	The Cosmic Christ will be recognized and the universal principle of love will be lived. The result will be "to produce that future scientific religion of *light* which will enable man to fulfill the command of the historical Christ to permit his light to shine forth."[1]

[1]Adapted from A.A. Bailey, *Esoteric Psychology*, Vol. I, 362.

Sixth Ray (Piscean age)	Seventh Ray (Aquarian age)
The use of ostentatious meaninglessness for personal ritual.	Meaningful simplified ritual to convey the energies of service.
The appearance of the modern science of psychology; belief in the Soul has become widespread.	Psychology will be advanced to include esoteric psychology; *knowledge* of the Soul will become widespread.
Necessary separateness and pronounced individualism.	Organizing power and group process.
External authority.	Internal authority.
Vertical political structures.	Horizontal political structures.
Economic domination and manipulation.	Economic sharing and equality.
Separation of spirit and matter.	Blending of spirit and matter.
God transcendent.	God immanent.

IV

THE SOUL

The Seven Planes and the Human Trinity.

The basic trinity of life, consciousness and form (Purpose, Plan and Activity) exists in every human as in every other being, macrocosmic and microcosmic. In Man it is called Spirit, Soul and Personality. In esoteric language the 'Spirit', which is for many a vague and nebulous designation, is sometimes called the 'Monad'.

7 Planes of Human Existence	Human Trinity
Divine or Logoic	
Monadic — — — — — — —	Monad
Atmic	
Buddhic ⎫	Soul
Mental Higher ⎬	
Lower ⎫	
Astral ⎬	Personality
Etheric-Physical ⎭	

The *Divine* is the life of the Planetary Logos or Divinity.

The *Monad* is a spark of the divine or a cell within the planetary body. It is the deepest or highest level of individuality attainable by a Soul-centered consciousness. Master D.K. (Djwhal Kuhl) says that there are fifty billion human monads in existence, only ten percent of which are at this time in incarnation. Who are we to quibble with that assertion?

While the Monad—the word itself means 'one'—is a unity, the second aspect, the *Soul*, is a trinity. It is composed of atmic substance (Spiritual Will), buddhic substance (spiritual Love) and higher manas [mind] (spiritual Light/intelligent activity). The Soul is both the *result* of the Monad assuming form in the lower three worlds as a personality, and the *cause* of the lower three worlds of personality.

In a broad sense there is only one Soul or simply 'Soul', meaning 'consciousness.' Every being, however small or great, has and is consciousness; it is mind which separates this one consciousness into different kinds, such as mineral consciousness, animal consciousness, human consciousness or Soul consciousness. It is an arbitrary division we use to facilitate communication and mental understanding which will eventually be transcended when we can experience the unity of all consciousness beyond the mind.

When the impersonal human Soul casts itself into form it creates a threefold *personality*. The lower mental, as a reflection of the atmic, contains the personal will. The astral, containing personal love, is a reflection of the buddhic. The physical is a reflection of the higher Mental and is the plane of personal activity. The personal nature of will, love and activity are necessary vehicles to anchor their higher counterparts in form and matter, the essential means whereby redemption or spiritualization of matter occurs. Through experience and the awareness of higher dimensions which comes from experience, this personal will, love and activity begin more and more to become impersonal, inclusive expressions of the Divine Plan embodied in the Soul.

In the journey of consciousness expansion, we move through the levels of experiencing the personality before becoming Soul-conscious. The work of integrating the personality with the Soul is referred to as *building the Antahkarana*, a Sanskrit word which is translated to mean 'The Rainbow Bridge' or 'The Bridge/Link/Channel of Light.' This is the lower bridge. Once consciousness is dominantly centered in the Soul, the higher bridge or Antahkarana is then built, linking the trinity of man into one functioning whole.

The development of inclusiveness and the expansion of consciousness is not strictly a linear process, but it does develop and expand in stages. We must always bear in mind that regardless of which stage one is experiencing, the whole being—including all potential—is present and having an effect on the particular stage of experience.

Expansion of consciousness, on the other hand, proceeds in a cyclic fashion, viewed from the perspective of many lifetimes. We can gain a certain level of expertise and control at a lower plane, but there comes a point beyond which we cannot go unless we advance to a higher level. When we gain a modicum of control at a higher level, we are then capable of returning to the lower level to develop it further. Every advance is followed by a necessary retreat; every ascent leads to a temporary descent. No part can be perfected until the whole is mastered because the part must become the whole, the whole being the potential latent within every part.

Because of this it is very misleading to judge a person's overall spiritual status by observing the current level of focus. One might, for example, be focused for several years on the astral plane, going through a variety of emotional experiences. Casual observation might lead one to conclude that the astral is as far as this Soul has advanced, when in fact the person may have achieved (perhaps in previous lives) a much higher level of consciousness, but has temporarily returned to the astral level to learn to express the higher attainment of love, understanding or power through the emotional level.

Bodies

Each of the seven planes of existence are dimensions of reality which can be experienced. In order to consciously participate in the energy of a dimension, one requires a body through which to register impressions and to act upon the energies of that dimension. A *body* is a coherent field of energy held together around an individuality and activated from its potential state by the development of consciousness on a given plane. The body is a vehicle through which an entity can function. Each of us has seven bodies, corresponding to the seven planes. Some of these are merely potential, while some are in the process of being activated and others are active enough to be used somewhat reliably. Our physical body, for example, became activated through incarnation and we can use it more or less well. It is not perfect because it is only a part of us, the whole of which is not yet perfected. Most of humanity also has its emotional body activated, having been stimulated into activity during the last root-race, the Atlantean. We are now, in this present root-race, activating the mental body. It is obvious, however, that we have not gained as much control of the mental body as we have of the physical. For example, we find it much easier to sit in a chair for an hour or two, than to concentrate our minds on a particular issue for the same length of time. There are some more advanced members of humanity who are now developing their Soul bodies, activating the higher Mind, the Intuition and Spiritual Will. These are the Initiates of the human race.

The relative perfection of the personality bodies is attained as the Soul bodies come into conscious control.

—When the *higher mind* can be used at will the physical body functions harmoniously and to the fullness of its capacities because the energies of the higher mind, which are Light and Intelligent Activity, directly affect the etheric subplanes of the physical. These etheric subplanes are the subtle creators of the more dense aspects of the physical body. (The thoughts generated by the *lower mind* directly influence the gaseous, liquid and solid components of the physical body. Because of this cause and effect relationship between lower mind and physical body, we experience physically the direct results of the quality of our thoughts. In this context we can see the immediate cause of health, disease and accidents.)

—When we can consciously use the *intuition,* the astral body reaches a relative perfection. This enables us to express unconditional love through our feeling nature, rather than emotionally reacting in a selfish, possessive way.

—When the substance of the *atmic plane* is consciously contacted we have Spiritual or Divine Will. The personal will of the lower mind then yields to the higher will and reasons in light of that will. Thought is then a product of the higher purpose rather than an unconscious result of conditioned sense experience and personal desire.

Those who have embarked on a spiritual quest—by whatever name it may be called—are, in one way or another, attempting to develop Soul consciousness and to activate the Soul bodies, consequently perfecting the expression of the esoteric individuality through the personality or exoteric individuality. To facilitate this process of growth a deeper knowledge of all these bodies would be immensely useful. Because there is a more direct cause and effect relationship from 'the top down' rather than from 'the bottom up' we will consider the Soul and its nature before discussing the personality bodies.

Soul

There is an incredible array of words that either refer to the Soul or mean the same as Soul. The words used either reflect some type of bias, such as religious or psychological, or serve to emphasize some particular perspective. But regardless of the word used, the reality of the Soul can only be known through direct experience. The Soul is formless but words are forms; as such they are only indicators that may help to point the way to possible experience or serve to communicate the incommunicable.

The following are some synonyms used for the "Soul". They give some indication as to some of the characteristics and qualities of the Soul:

> The Soul; the Ego; the Self; the One Self; the Higher Self; the Spiritual Self; the One; the Inner Ruler; the God within; the Inner Reality; the Divine Inner Ruler; the Inner Spiritual Sun; the Divine Indweller; the Master Within the Heart; the Indwelling Flame; the Inner God; the

Christ Within; the Christ Principle; the Individuality; the Divine
Reality; the Real Man; the Thinker; the Spiritual Thinker; the Solar
Angel; the Angel; the Angel of the Presence; the Jewel; the Son of the
Father; the Flame of Spirit; the Developing Point; the Agnishvattas; the
Son of Mind; the Mediating Principle; the Triangles; the Director; the
Onlooking Unity; the Observer; the Onlooker; the Divine Perceiver;
the Beholder; the Watcher; the Interpreter.[1]

The fact that there are so many words from a variety of traditions and
schools of thought, lends credence to the existence of the Soul. Its reality
cannot be proven by materialistic reasoning any more than can the
existence of compassion, beauty, unconditional love, or any quality; but it
can be experienced, and through experience, can be known to be real.

The highly self-conscious individual is aware that there is a doer
behind the doing, a feeler behind the feeling and a thinker behind the
thinking—that there is an entity experiencing and directing these
activities of the personality. It is this entity which we call the Soul.

When we experience the Soul within ourselves and others, or within
nature, we are always struck by the inherent beauty of the being. In fact,
whenever beauty is recognized it is the Soul which is touched. That inner
beauty is frequently experienced in people as unconditional love. Beauty
and Love are, for the majority of people, the easiest way to apprehend the
Soul because these two qualities are readily experienced in the astral body,
which is a common level of experience for most of humanity which is
decidedly emotionally polarized.

The Soul is composed of a trinity of differentiated substance—atmic,
buddhic and manasic. As such it embodies the three principles of Power,
Love and Light.

Soul Power is the immediate *purpose* of the incarnated entity as well as the
ultimate *purpose* that the Soul serves within the body of the Planetary
Being. We as individuals can know our immediate and ultimate purpose

---

[1]Bailey, A.A., *The Soul, the Quality of Life—A Compilation*, 23.

for being only when we become conscious at the atmic level. Then we know the Divine Will; until then we follow our personal will.

Soul Power is an extension of the esoteric center called *Shamballa*—the head center of the Planetary Logos. It is also a manifestation of the first *universal law of synthesis*.

Soul Love is the plan for our individual lives and the *Plan* of the Planetary Life. It is this love which gives *meaning* to everything. Only by developing and using intuition and by experiencing unconditional love (which we can only do with intuitive awareness) can we discover meaning. When we find the true meaning of any event or any being, we touch the plan of love which is causing the event or being to be the way it is. This is true even in a so-called negative expression where that plan is not consciously recognized and where love is not manifesting. When Soul Love first stimulates inertia into activity the result is invariably 'negative'. Through working with the negative, the positive is discovered. Eventually the synthesis of the two is produced which is a direct and meaningful experience of Soul Love.

Soul Love is an extension of the esoteric center called *Hierarchy* (the Planetary Hierarchy or fifth kingdom of nature)—the *heart center* of the Planetary Logos. It is also a planetary and individual manifestation of the second universal law, which is the *law of attraction*.

Soul Light is the activity of the individual as well as the *Intelligence* or the entire *intelligent activity* of the Planetary Logos. For the individual the activity of the mental, astral and physical bodies is stimulated by this Light, even though we normally think of activity as purely physical. When activity is "lighted" it is intelligent, it has meaning and it serves the purpose. What gives Light the essential property of intelligence is its manasic substance which composes the higher mental plane where relationships are perceived and ideals are embodied. These ideals are formulated from universal ideas and are seeking expression into concrete reality as thoughts. When the light of consciousness from the Soul is not present, the activity is apparently meaningless and purposeless—although it can, in the long run, serve to bring a person into the Light.

The life and activity of the Planetary Logos is one of Light (symbolized by its third ray energy) because in its evolution as an entity it is polarized on, and functioning within, the lowest cosmic dimension known as the Cosmic Physical Plane. The physical plane is always characterized by activity. On the cosmic level of the physical where the Planetary Logos is focused, Light is always present and therefore all the activity taking place within Its body (the earth) is intelligent. Every one of the seven planes of our human constitution is a subdivision of the Cosmic Physical Plane. It follows then that each plane is filled with Light and is intelligent, capable of serving the evolving Planetary Being.

Soul Light is an extension of the esoteric center called *Humanity*—the *throat center* of the Planetary Logos. It is humanity's role to express the creative Purpose and Plan of this being. It is also a planetary and individual manifestation of the third universal law—the *Law of Economy*.

Soul Qualities

When we speak of Soul we refer to the dimension of *quality* rather than *quantity*. Qualities are the consciousness aspects of life and can be expressed on different levels, such as on Soul levels with more completeness or on personality levels with more self-serving motives and partiality.

A group of students studying the nature of the Soul composed the following list of Soul qualities.

Joy	Clarity	Spiritual Indifference
Beauty	Inspiration	Abundance
Love	Healing	Sharing
Gratitude	Purification	Energy
Peace	Transformation	Daring
Harmony	Humor	Spontaneity
Serenity	Gentleness	Focus
Compassion	Oneness	Generosity
Forgiveness	Harmlessness	Good Will
Honesty	Mindfulness	Will-to-good
Strength	Steadfastness	Courage
Tranquillity	Simplicity	Communication
Patience	Openness	Tolerance
Enthusiasm	Endurance	Synthesis
Purpose	Brotherhood	Purity
Integrity	Wisdom	Long-suffering
Light	Certainty	Will
Infinity	Empathy	Limitlessness
Grace	Liberation	Bliss
Freedom	Surrender	Truth
Serenity	Discrimination	Power
Detachment	Discipline	Responsibility
Radiance	Understanding	Intuition
Devotion	Unity	Inclusiveness
Service	Creativity	
Trust	Self-sufficiency	

Summary of Teaching on the Soul

The following statements will serve as seed thoughts for reflection and meditation as well as give a fuller picture of the nature and characteristics of who we are as Souls.

1. *There is only 'Soul'.* When we are approaching the Soul in our consciousness but still rooted in our personality to a great extent, we will perceive and experience Soul as individual. However, once the consciousness significantly shifts into the level of Soul we will experience it in its oneness and all-inclusiveness.

2. *Soul is the middle principle* between Spirit and form, and therefore the principle of all relationships. True relationship implies conscious presence. It implies interplay between life and activity. The middle principle is consciousness or Soul. In human relationships it is the Soul which chooses the relationships we experience. We may think that we, in our personality, make the choices of our friends, our mates, our loved ones, but in fact these choices are always made at Soul levels. The reason or the purpose for all relationships is to promote growth in consciousness.

3. *Soul is the unity of consciousness* which we call Love or Christ. The Christ referred to here is the Cosmic Christ or the Christ Principle.

4. *Soul is the second aspect of divinity,* although it is the manifestation of the trinity—Will, Love, Light.

5. *Soul is the energy* of Atma, Buddhi, and Higher Manas.

6. *Soul is formless,* but relates to form and creates form.

7. *Soul can be related to* through visions, ideas, dreams and symbols, and can be sensed through our weaknesses, resistances and feelings; it can also be experienced through our talents and our strengths.

8. *Soul is potential.* It is potential actualization. When human potential is referred to it is always a reference to the Soul which can be awakened and stimulated within the personality. Every potential that is developed is an expression of the Soul.

9. *The Soul's energies can be perceived* as qualities, characteristics and virtues.

10. *The lowest aspect of the Soul* itself on the higher mental plane *is the causal body,* repository of the permanent atoms and cause of all that appears in form.

The *causal body* is an esoteric reference to the lowest aspect of the Soul itself on the higher mental plane. It is here that the essence of the incarnated life is registered and stored, and from here that the new personality is created.

The highest (first) subplane of every dimension or body is called the *atomic* subplane or level. These atoms are, in a way, composed of the Monadic life, thereby carrying the purpose characteristic of the Monad. They also carry the ray energy for the bodies. It is this atomic level which is the blueprint as well as the creative force for the lower subplanes within the respective dimension or body. For example, the atomic level of the etheric-physical dimension is the 1st etheric sub-plane. It contains the blueprint for all that manifests in the lower etheric levels as well as in the dense physical body. According to this atomic nature, which is uniquely individual, the physical body takes shape, develops, grows and experiences. Each of the bodies follows this same pattern.

Within the atomic level of each body we find what some esotericists call 'the permanent atoms.' These are the most refined atoms of each body and while they do create, as already noted, they also store, are affected by, and their quality altered somewhat by, the life experiences. *It is not the form of the experiences which is retained but the essence or quality of the mental, emotional and physical life as lived.* This retained essence is carried within the causal body to color and affect subsequent experiences within the mental, astral and physical bodies. In this structure we have the mechanism of how we create our own future. The process just described is not limited to this life alone. It also provides continuity from one lifetime to another.

11. *The Soul is the meaning* of all that happens in manifestation.

12. *Soul is the stage of synthesis* for all that occurs in the lower three worlds. This means that the perfection of all that exists in the lower three worlds is Soul life.

13. *Soul is the eye of the Monad.* The Monad, the highest state of individuality that we are (the Spirit), seeks to express itself as a divine being within the worlds of matter. It does this through the Soul which is but an extension of the Monad, just as the personality is an extension of the Soul. The Soul is that consciousness whereby the Monad can see into the lower worlds. It cannot approach the lower worlds without the intermediate step that the Soul provides. It is the attractive force of the created universe, holding all forms together, a manifestation of the second Universal Law—*the Law of Attraction.*

14. *Soul is the force of evolution* itself.

15. *Soul is that which gives every form its characteristics,* qualities, differences and uniqueness.

16. *Soul is the principle of intelligence and the principle of sentiency.* It is said that the Soul is to the personality what the etheric body is to the dense

physical body. While the physical body's senses are truly within the etheric counterpart and only exist as organs within the physical body, the sensing of a person is done by the etheric body. Behind these senses there is a principle that allows them to function. This is the principle of sentiency which is the Soul that is within that body. For example, when a person dies the Soul leaves the physical body. Because of its absence the senses no longer function. This same principle of sentiency is found within the emotional or astral body and it is because of the Soul's presence that we are able to sense or feel with our astral body and with our emotions. Our minds can only function intelligently when the Soul is present within them; and we are only intelligent to the degree of that Soul presence.

17. *The Soul exists outside of time and space on its own plane, but relates to time and space.* The Soul, not the personality, is the reincarnating entity. From its perspective all incarnations are simultaneous. Each incarnation is but an opportunity for the Soul or consciousness to gain experience or mastery of the different energies of the lower worlds and thus restore these worlds to the whole of which they are a part. This work of restoration, often called *redemption*, is simply bringing full consciousness into the lower worlds according to their nature and according to their capacity.

18. *The Soul reaches in two directions* simultaneously—to the form and to the Monad.

19. *The Soul expresses itself in cycles,* following the basic pulse of outgoing and ingoing, of expression and impression, of creation and destruction, of integration and disintegration.

20. *The Soul embodies the Plan and knows the Purpose.*

21. *The Soul can work in all three lower worlds* simultaneously and remain karmically free from the results of such work because it is detached. The Soul is the Path even though when we walk the spiritual path we may consider ourselves to be walking as personalities toward the Soul. Walking the Path is becoming the Soul or being the Soul.

22. *All problems, challenges, diseases, are a result of selfishness* and lack of alignment between the personality and Soul (Love).

23. *The Soul expresses itself through radiation or emanation.* Parallel to this is the way in which the new etheric body is created, into which, as into a mold, the new physical body is built.

24. *The Soul is a vortex of twelve energies* held together by the Purpose and the Will of the Monad. This vortex is symbolized as a lotus called the *Egoic Lotus.* This lotus is composed in the following way. There are three

outer tiers of petals and one tier of three inner petals. Each tier of the outer petals is composed of three petals. The outermost tier is called the *knowledge petals*. This is the first part of the Egoic Lotus to unfold or open as the aspiring personality seeks knowledge of, and union with the Soul. The next tier of petals to unfold is the *love petals*. These begin to unfold as a person begins to love others for their own sake and true love becomes a reality. The third tier of petals to unfold before the inner realm is touched is the *sacrifice petals*. These unfold as the individual dedicates himself in sacrifice to the good of the whole for manifestation of the Plan. The inner three petals that are said to be unfolded around the brilliant point of electric fire called the Jewel are sometimes called *Sacrifice, Enthusiasm and Nobility*. Each of these petals contains one of the three permanent atoms found in the Higher Mental, the Buddhic and the Atmic bodies of the Initiate.

25. Some of the *Soul's primary characteristics* are suggested by these words: inclusiveness, detachment, love, intuition, will-to-good, freedom, joy, serenity, sacrifice, service, sharing, wisdom, responsibility.

26. *When the Soul life is awakened* there are various effects to be seen in the personality life. A person begins to experience more conflict between different values and different perspectives. One becomes more sensitive to ideas with an increased flexibility and broadmindedness. Detachment from previous interests gradually develops along with an increased creativity.

27. *Soul is group conscious.*

Group Consciousness

There is a natural progression from individual consciousness to self-consciousness to group consciousness to God consciousness. These are the steps of an evolving inclusiveness that mark the journey toward wholeness in which every being becomes increasingly responsible and useful in the unfolding Plan and Purpose of life. There exists today a notable degree of human self-consciousness such that we can speak meaningfully of the next step in our evolution—group consciousness.

When we speak of 'group' we tend to think of a collection of individuals being together or working together. While that is part of group consciousness it is only a possible effect or by-product of group consciousness. Groups exist for a variety of reasons, many of which are self-serving, working more or less harmoniously together and cooperating with each other to a greater or lesser degree to achieve some stated objectives which in some way help only the members of the group.

There are ecology groups, peace groups, animal rights groups, social groups, recreation groups, etc. Such gathering together of individuals with common goals is a necessary and useful step toward developing group consciousness.

An esoteric group, by definition, is a group on the inner mental and intuitive planes. The members are linked subjectively, while possibly also linked through an external group. The purpose of esoteric groups is inevitably to serve humanity as a bridge or link between less inclusive and more inclusive ways of being. This involves being able to demonstrate non-egotistical relationships.

Group consciousness is characterized by:

—an awareness of some aspect of the Plan;
—a sensitivity to a real need outside of oneself;
—a desire to serve the good of the whole;
—a willingness to sacrifice personal gain and interest for group good;
—an effort to be an instrument of transformation;
—an aspiration to be a cause of change rather than a manipulator of effects;
—a striving to improve one's own ability to be in contact with higher spheres of energy;
—a demonstration of loyalty, faithfulness, discipline of life, efficiency in work and a sense of responsibility, trust, discrimination and endurance;
—an ability to embrace and carry a vision;
—a centeredness of being and awareness in the Soul.

Soul consciousness is, by definition, group consciousness. When we are self-conscious we perceive the Soul as individual because we are viewing the Soul from the level of personality where we recognize we 'have' a Soul. When we become that Soul we then see that:

—we *have* a personality.
—we *are* Soul and are one with all Souls.

It is this oneness which gives rise to all the characteristics of group consciousness. With the consequent diminished sense of separatism the individual loses egotism and lives for the whole. Sacrifice becomes second nature and service flows spontaneously from such a way of being.

Group consciousness is an inner reality which has an effect, direct or indirect, on outer plane activity. The inner group is linked with Hierarchy and its work in directing the unfoldment of humanity into greater love and greater light.

To work effectively at the level of group consciousness the individual and the group need to become consciously aware of:

—group purpose
—group plan
—group activity

As the members of the group become increasingly familiar with the level of their consciousness they will develop group telepathy. The telepathic link will begin with the subtle communication of the Soul between the members, and evolve to the level of being telepathically impressed by the Plan, and its embodiment in the loving intelligence of its custodians, the Hierarchy.

As we enter the Aquarian age with seventh ray influence we are increasingly exposed to its power for right relations and service. Its influence infuses matter with spirit, the particular with the universal. In doing so it reveals the essence or the Soul, thereby assisting us to set up group rhythms and group relationships through which we become more sensitive to impression from the higher sources. Joined with others at the level of group consciousness we are connected in mind and in heart.

Genuine, unconditional love, of course, is the essential bond that unites people and enables them to serve unselfishly. It is *the* facilitator of group consciousness and group endeavor.

Methods of Developing Soul Consciousness

Although the development of Soul and group consciousness is a slow process there are many things we can choose to do which will speed up the desired growth.

a. Discover, reveal and implement *quality* in all things. Quality is the Soul. When we show our own positive qualities we are manifesting our Soul. When we have quality relationships, even in the briefest exchanges, we relate to the Soul of the other. When we do work carefully and responsibly we can reveal the Soul. When we look for the essential reason behind events we are seeking the Soul.

b. Develop the faculty of *abstract thought* or power to link up with the higher mind. The higher mind is the causal body—an aspect of the Soul. Abstract thought is thinking within this body. Philosophical, metaphysical and esoteric reading, discussion and listening all contribute to this level of thought and exercise the ability to grasp and express the principles, causes and influences of phenomena.

c. Discover *meaning* behind reality, behind the appearance or form. The meaning of anything is its soul.

d. Think *causally* to deeper and deeper levels. Every level which is not the absolute is caused by the preceding higher level. The physical is caused by the astral which, in turn, is caused by the lower mental, which is caused by the higher mental, etc.—all the way back to Original Cause. The reversal of thinking from effect to cause leads one initially to the Soul, and eventually to the Monad. Thinking causally extends our previous limits of perception, progressively impelling us to more comprehensive awareness.

e. Grow in *love*, and express that love through giving and compassion. Love is the unifying energy of consciousness emanating from the Soul. Expressing love to our greatest capacity even in the smallest of things opens the channel from personality to Soul.

f. Intentionally *link* with the Soul. This can be done quickly and easily by a mere thought of being the Soul or being under the guidance of the Soul. The mental intention can be visualized as a link of powerful, loving light connecting the two centers of identity—Soul and personality. The intention can be verbalized in an affirmation or mantram (repetitive saying) such as: "I am the Soul," "I am the responsible cause," "I am being divinely guided and am therefore protected and safe," "I am Love, I am Light, I am Power." In the book, *Rainbow Bridge* by Two Disciples, there is an effective affirmation called 'The Soul Mantram.' It is:

I am the Soul.
I am the Light Divine.
I am Love.
I am Will.
I am Fixed Design.

g. Practice a form of *meditation* in which there is a deliberate intention to align with the Soul.

h. Develop the 'habit' of *service*. Service is the first sign in the individual that the Soul is expressing itself through the individual's thoughts or actions. Service is an attitude of unconditional love responding to need. It may or may not externalize in action. What distinguishes true service from only apparent service activity is the attitude of unconditional love, selfless response to need, willing sacrifice of personal desire, and absence of judgment. Service can be present as a Soul energy in absolutely any situation and in every task, however small or private.

i. Live a life of *virtue*. Virtues are the qualities of the Soul characterizing action. Attempting to exercise such qualities as patience, perseverance tolerance, acceptance and forgiveness are efforts at attracting Soul into action.

j. Listen to the all-loving *guidance* of the Soul. The Soul controls the life whether or not we are mentally conscious of this direction. When we are listening to our own personal, selfish desires we may temporarily be resisting the Soul's guidance. When we become conscious of the Soul's loving presence, we try to respond to its impulses to be led into right action and into the true state of our inner being. It is the only reliable guide we have.

The Soul is the point of contact with the 'eternal now.' It is always in the present moment, in contrast to the mind which is more often than not either in the past or in the future. Everything we need is *in* the present and *is* present. By following the guidance of the Soul we know what we need to know and we have what we need to have. Soul functions in the moment in a spontaneous, creative way. It is true. It brings peace and serenity. It penetrates clearly through the fog of illusions. It balances distorted perspectives. It heals the wounds of conflict. It gives meaning and shows purpose.

Group Work

Group consciousness is the expression of Buddhic consciousness and therefore requires an intuitive alignment or at-one-ment. It is the level of consciousness which is equated with Love in its (for us) highest attainable sense. For those of us striving for group consciousness we may see it practically as the synthesis of thought present in a unified group—synthesized around, and devoted to, the group work.

We can work towards the higher state of group consciousness by creating the means whereby that consciousness can grow. The following suggestions should prove helpful.

a. Every member of a group must take *full responsibility* for the plans and purpose of the group—its ideas, thoughts, objectives, intentions and activities.

b. Each group member should have *equal responsibility* and voice within the group. There should be no superior or inferior positions to which members are assigned, elected or for which they could volunteer.

c. The tendency toward uniformity needs to be strictly avoided. Uniformity is an external conformity that does not respect differences. Unity is an ideal, but the way to manifest that ideal in group is through *unanimity*—the fostering of the *same spirit*. The diversity of ideas, ray-types and approaches are necessary in a group for the completeness and wholeness of the group Soul and for providing a variety of approaches to express the Soul and Spirit of the group.

d. Group structure is to be *horizontal* rather than vertical. In a vertical group structure there are the leaders and the followers; and there is frequently a power struggle to determine who the leaders will be. Vertical structures tend to arise where self-esteem is lacking. In a horizontal structure the leadership is provided by the group Soul as it is capable of embodying aspects of the Hierarchical Plan. In groups where there are more intuitively developed individuals there will be a tendency to depend on them for direction and guidance. However, they should exercise a great deal of discretion so that their contributions to the group do not minimize the valid input from every other member, and do not foster dependency. The role of the more developed is primarily to raise the level of the entire group through their presence and vision rather than through their direction.

e. Conclusions and decisions for the group are to be arrived at, not through imposing the will of the majority or of the most powerful, but through arriving at a group consensus. A *consensus* is achieved when:

—the spirit of the facts or objectives has been sufficiently revealed;

—all the members have attuned to that spirit and found it to be suitable and acceptable.

Reaching consensus may at first seem lengthy and onerous, but eventually it will prove to be quicker and more efficient than the usual debating, arguing and power playing that is characteristic of rule by majority. If all members are to take equal and full responsibility for the entire group, consensus is the only way of supporting individual responsibility.

f. The presence of *doubt* in the minds of a few can hinder the work of the group. If anyone has doubts and reservations about decisions made these should be expressed and discussed so that the group energy can be strong and effectively directed. Doubt blocks the clarity of expression.

g. Personal ambition, even if it be spiritual, has an undermining and destructive effect on the group. Open and honest communication about personal *motives* needs to be supported. Even group motive must frequently be checked. Once motives deteriorate the group can become useless as a center of service, functioning in its own self-serving interests rather than as a vehicle for elevating consciousness.

h. Developing a *group vision* is a priority. The vision is the embodiment of that part of the Plan that the group can grasp. It is the fuel and power for group unity and effective action. Refine this vision from time to time, keeping it alive and ever-present in the group mind, but changing it as needs and opportunities change. When the group vision has been fulfilled either the group will no longer continue to exist as such or a new vision must be sought.

i. '*The Highest*' should be the objective of every group. When differences are present resolution can usually come about by all reaching a little higher—to the Soul, where harmony exists. Respect each other and recognize that the differences are but different aspects of truth. The highest possibility should be sought in every situation.

j. While the idealism found in groups is necessary and useful, *practicality* is equally necessary and useful. The group may be very good at grasping principles, discussing ideals and deciding what needs to be done, but that is only half the required job. It must be expressed in some way, often physically. Doing the job requires the stimulation of possible inertia or physical laziness and developing skill in-action. This may require willpower or special training, but for the most part usually requires only the doing. Through doing, skill will develop and learning will take place.

k. A common fault found in many groups is the tendency to *not follow through* with one's verbal commitments. People say they will do something and then not do it or do it partially or poorly. The consequences are always unfortunate for the group. The group needs to be able to honor each member and depend upon each member's commitments. The irresponsibility of some members increases the responsibility or duties of others, setting the stage for inequality and lack of trust within the group.

l. When a group gathers for a meeting or a task, take a few minutes to *link up* intentionally with the Soul, the purpose, the vision. Draw upon the Love that strengthens the group.

m. The group is more important than its members as individuals. Let your own interests be temporarily set aside for the *group good* when they are irrelevant to group purpose.

The Seven Laws of Group Work

These seven laws are the septenary life of being as Soul—macrocosmic and microcosmic. They apply to the Soul consciousness of the Planetary Being, but for now we will consider them from the point of view of human application.

Law 1. The Law of Sacrifice.

Once there is a realization of greater wholeness, that which has been realized or achieved is renounced. 'Sacrifice' means 'to make whole, holy, healthy.' There is both a letting go of that which hinders further movement as well as a using of that which has been realized to serve the greater. This is crucifixion, the basic law of all group work, the potent symbol of Love, and the symbol of the Third Initiation when the illusion of separation is transcended.

Law 2. The Law of Magnetic Impulse.

Soul is a magnetic energy. This law governs the attractiveness of Soul to Soul, the Self in all. Sometimes called "the first step towards marriage," this law results in eventual union between the group and the individual and the union between groups.

Law 3. The Law of Service.

The individual identifies with the group interest and disidentifies from personal interests. It is the positive life of the group which facilitates this.

Law 4. The Law of Repulsion.

This is the ability and the necessity to throw off or refuse to contact any energy deemed inimical to group activity. This is not a negative rejection or denial, but has the effect of lovingly furthering the interest of the repulsed unit and of driving this unit closer to its own center. An example of this could be seen if a group decides not to accept an individual as a member because that person would be drawn too far away from the work he/she really needed to be doing and the group might be a substitute or escape from personal responsibility. This law is a law of service.

Law 5. The Law of Group Progress.

Sometimes called 'The Law of Elevation', this law concerns group realization and the expansions of consciousness which take place within a group and within each member or unit of a group. As each individual is expanded or raised so is the group.

Law 6. The Law of Expansive Response and Law 7. The Law of the Lower Four.

These two laws concern group activity, primarily on the astral and mental planes. Their true meaning and relevance is beyond our understanding.

The Transformation of Humanity[1]

There is currently a great experiment in process in group formation, development and expression. This group experiment is being conducted by the Hierarchy of Masters and is involving many human beings on the

---

[1]Adapted from Bailey, A.A., *Discipleship in the New Age*, Vol. I, 35-40.

inner planes. These individuals are those who have developed sufficient sensitivity that they are able to respond to impression by Hierarchy and who are capable of working in mental matter. They comprise ten groups, often referred to as 'seed groups.' Their names and functions are:

1. *Telepathic communicators.* This group is receptive to impression from both Hierarchy and from each other within the group; they may be called the custodians of group purpose and therefore relate to all the other groups. They work largely on the mental plane, through thought matter and with both the reception and direction of thought currents. They develop the ability to communicate beyond words, and develop methods to increase the effectiveness of all communication. They direct efforts towards Soul to Soul communication on the higher levels of the mental plane. This necessitates the consciousness connections among Soul, mind and brain. They also develop communication between mind and mind— pure mental telepathy. This requires personality integration so that the mind and brain function harmoniously together and as a single expression.

2. *Trained observers.* Their objective is to see clearly through all events in and through space and time by developing the intuition. They work largely on the astral plane to dissipate glamor and to bring illumination to humanity. This is the development of communication between the intuitive plane of illumination and the astral plane, the level of glamor. The trained observers have the task of dispelling world illusion (of which glamor is an example on the astral plane) through the pouring in of light.

3. *Magnetic healers.* The focus of their work will be on the etheric body. There is work to be done on the intelligent transmission of energy to various parts of the personality—mental, emotional and physical— through the right organization and proper circulation of appropriate energies. The primary work is to function as intermediary among the higher planes of Soul energy, intuitional energy or will energy and the personality with its disturbances. All healing ultimately involves the alignment between the form and the essence of that form which is the Soul, as all disease or illness is but indication of misalignment. All healing work in the Aquarian age will be group rather than individual work. Magnetic healers must learn to work as Souls and not as individuals.

4. *Educators of the new age.* They will work to bring in the new type of education, with the emphasis upon the building of the Antahkarana and upon the use of the mind. They will act as communicators and as transmitters of knowledge and wisdom. They function as the intermediary between the higher mind and the lower mind. Their concern is the linking of the higher mind, the Soul and the lower mind so that there can

be established a group Antahkarana between the kingdom of Souls (the fifth kingdom) and the world of humanity (the fourth kingdom).

5. *Political organizers.* Here the work is in the realm of human government, dealing with the problems of civilization and the establishment of right relationships among nations. This is largely first ray work, embodying the method whereby the divine Will works out in the consciousness of races and nations.

6. *The workers in the field of religion.* Their work proceeds toward the formulation of the new world religion. It is a work of loving synthesis and emphasizes the unity and fellowship of the religious spirit. The work is along the lines of the second ray of love-wisdom which is that of the World Teacher, known in the west as the Christ.

7. *The scientific servers.* They will reveal the essential spirituality of all scientific work which is motivated by love of humanity and its welfare. Science and spirituality will be bridged and this primarily when etheric vision is developed and is commonly possessed. The aim is to show that all is divine in both essence and form. This demonstration can initially revolve around the issue of reincarnation, showing that the personality is a vehicle for a reincarnating Soul.

8. *The psychologists.* This group is concerned with the revelation of the fact of the Soul and works towards the new psychology which will be based on the seven ray types and esoteric astrology. The dynamics of Soul-personality relationship will be revealed. They will also act as transmitters of illumination between groups of thinkers and as illuminators of group thought. They transmit energy from one thought center to another and, above all else, they transmit the energy of ideas. The world of ideas exists as archetypes and universal principles; this group needs to contact and assimilate these ideas and then transmit them for implementation by humanity.

9. *The group of financiers and economists.* Working with the energies and forces of commerce, they deal with the law of supply and demand and with that great principle of sharing which is a manifestation of the third universal law of economy governing right activity of the divine purpose. The principle of sharing is a Soul quality or energy and must govern economic relations; hence their work of relating Soul with Soul.

10. *Group of creative workers.* Creativity is the linking and blending of life and form, so the work of this group is between the third aspect of divinity, the creative aspect, as it expresses itself through the creative work and in response to the thought world—the first aspect of divinity: life. Their work is to bring the divine Plan into the physical plane.

V

SPIRITUAL DEVELOPMENT

Since esoteric living and philosophy emphasize spiritual development, it is mandatory to put this in a perspective which deals with the essence of spiritual development.

Any kind of development, whether it be economic, political, religious, psychological, artistic or of any human activity, is spiritual when it involves the application of the universal principles and laws of life. In more practical terms this means that when the qualities of the Soul, such as inclusiveness, beauty, goodness and love, are present there is an expansion of the form or part into a greater, meaningful and life-supporting whole. This is spiritual development. 'Spiritual' is unfortunately too often equated only with 'religious'. It is in fact a component of every field of human activity as represented by the seven rays of life and consciousness. We might also say that what is evolutionary is spiritual, since both are movements toward the whole.

In terms of personal development we must first recognize that each person has a basic personality character which cannot change to be some other type of character. In esoteric psychology the character is defined by the dynamics of the interacting rays which constitute it. But what can change within every character, and therefore also its behavior, is the emphasis put upon the different aspects of the character. Each one has a complete range of qualities or characteristics from the completely negative to the outstandingly positive. In an evolutionary sense everyone progresses from the negative to the positive. We can increasingly choose the positive over the negative until it appears that the negative no longer exists. It *does* continue to exist but as an empty shell or latent possibility from which the life has been removed and given to the positive. With the positive emphasis becoming the dominant way of being, the negative and positive duality is eventually synthesized. The swing between the two is transcended and a higher harmonic level of the reality they represent is achieved. This level is that of the Soul. Only when this level is attained is there true spiritual development and change in consciousness.

Spiritual development is not possible without paying attention to the needs of the personality. The *ultimate need* of the personality is subordination to, and unity with, Soul. But the *immediate needs* of the personality may be quite different, although these must be seen in light of the ultimate need. You may, for example, need to learn more physical practicality or you may need to improve your physical well-being. You may need to learn where and how you are emotionally blocked or out of control, or how to express your emotions more suitably. You may need more mental development, or need to learn how to concentrate, analyze or think logically, or you may generally require more mental discipline.

Spiritual development occurs *through* the personality, not beyond it, because the personality—being the Soul's outer expression—is the means of accessing the Soul. The three bodies or three worlds of expression *are* the Soul in manifestation.

The Subconscious

The path to Soul union is as clear as the personal subconscious. If the subconscious is loaded with inhibitions, repressions, negatives or limitations—counter-productive, *accepted* patterns of thought and feeling—one is kept isolated and insulated from communication and communion with one's own true nature, the Soul. These patterns relate inevitably to egocentricity, selfishness, ego survival and separateness. They keep one from loving to the degree in which they are present. Love is the energy of union and is the basic requirement for spiritual development.

Learning to love helps to remove the hindering patterns. Or, conversely, removing the patterns leads to loving more.

Love makes no distinctions between self and other, for in love both are one. It is often said that we need to love ourselves *before* loving others. This is not true. If we love ourselves we do love others, and if we love others we love ourselves, because the "object" of our love is, in essence, neither self nor other but the deepest Self (Soul or God) or the total Other (Soul or God), and in that orientation, realized or not, there is no separation into "me" and "you".

Any attempt to communicate or contact any reality is colored, tainted or distorted by the condition of our subconscious. There is no authentic way of by-passing the subconscious in communication. Its distortions and limitations are responsible for our limited success in establishing deeper union in relationships with people, Soul, Self, God, nature, etc.

The patterns of the subconscious can be recognized by observing the limitations that manifest in our lives. Some of this limitation is a result of our ray composition, some is due to past life residue, and some is due to the experiences relating to this incarnation which begins at the time of conception. By far the most important areas that need to be dealt with are those which relate to the accumulation from pre-natal, infancy and childhood periods as these usually have the most effect in the present life.

In working with the subconscious we can make some changes once we recognize what is there; then counteract each element in turn. The important thing to keep in mind is that there be no further denial of an element or pattern once it is recognized, but to live with it, to co-exist with it in an accepting way. To accept it is to recognize that it exists for a valid reason. There was cause, and cause produces effect.

But now that the effect has been determined it can be dealt with. Until it is recognized it cannot be dealt with.

There are ways of breaking through the natural barrier or filter that exists between subconscious and conscious. Some ways are useful, some not. But more important is the speed and timing of the breaking through. If too much too fast is released, harm or confusion results. Then these effects have to be dealt with. Repeated use of some drugs can produce this effect, or immersion in certain "growth" processes that are followed at an inappropriate time in one's life.

For the open person seeking change and growth there is usually enough subconscious material emerging naturally that one does not have to force the process.

Meditation is also a releasing mechanism. Any form of meditation which is practical should always begin with attempted alignment with the higher (or Soul) so that what is released from the subconscious can more easily be integrated in light of the Soul or whole. Meditation should initially be done in small doses and preferably under the guidance of someone who is skilled at understanding inner processes because some of the subconscious content can be disturbing when it surfaces.

The subconscious is the source of motivation and impulse for most people. For others the source would be the Soul. Until one is totally Soul conscious, the Soul's direction and impulse filters through the subconscious and is colored by the subconscious.

The subconscious is the automatic recorder of all experience—external or internal, real or imaginary—and all thought. Emotion is triggered by a thought or experience affecting some area of the subconscious. All emotions therefore usually, if not always, begin with some thought that triggers something recorded in the subconscious. The existence of the subconscious is necessary for an unconscious person's survival. Hence, the emotions are also related to survival and, in their lower expression keep a person somewhat isolated and separate from others, the Soul and life.

If we wish to consciously affect the content of the subconscious we can:

—*Watch what we think*—think about what we want to condition us;

—*Watch what we imagine*—imagine that which leads to health and wholeness;

—*Think, imagine and affirm* through speech and action the way we choose to be. Try to align this aspiration, desire or choice with that of the Soul or simply with that which is consciously chosen to be, in some way, better.

This latter will lead to a possible conflict if what is consciously chosen is in direct contradiction to some pattern already existing in the subconscious. Lack of success in achieving what we consciously choose is always a sign of contradicting patterns existing in the subconscious.

We can *try* to proceed as if the inhibition were not there, but that does not always work, and it is too easy to fall into repression. It is far better to recognize and accept what is there and deal with it in some satisfactory way before attempting to go too far.

Our emotion-feelings are usually quite reliable in telling us if there is something blocking our movement forward in any chosen direction. These could be feelings of worthlessness, unworthiness, inferiority, guilt, shame, fear, etc.

Some people use hypnosis or self-hypnosis to carry out the changes they want when there is a subconscious block present. They might succeed temporarily because the hypnotic process can suppress the contrary subconscious urge and thus allow the new hypnotic suggestions to be the primary motivator.

The hypnosis process of suppression is ultimately not healthy because what is hypnotically or otherwise suppressed will continue to block the Soul's guidance to the conscious mind and heart, even though the personality-chosen outer behavior may be successfully altered.

True growth always leads to greater integration between essence and form, or, between Soul and personality. This implies the need to become more conscious or aware of what one is, in both essence and form. This expanding consciousness leads to becoming aware of unconscious elements in the subconscious and the Soul. Eventually all repressed and suppressed elements need to surface and be enveloped in consciousness.

To change the old obstructing patterns one needs to *become aware* of them and *remain aware* of them as long as they are affecting one. One must avoid excessive preoccupation with them because preoccupation indicates that one is not totally accepting the pattern.

Total acceptance of the limitation must follow awareness of the pattern. Once it is accepted it can then be worked with, sublimated and slowly dissipated through acting in an unlimited, uninhibited way, "as if" it did not exist. Awareness and acceptance in the light of the whole or Soul releases much of the power of the limiting pattern.

The limitations from conditioning that we find in the subconscious are often associated with fear. At the least they are joyless and dour—"heavy." So, when acting "as if" they do not exist, one must act lightly and joyfully. The power of joy for transmutation is indeed great. Joy is not only present naturally when there are no impediments that need to be dealt with, but especially and more genuinely when there are impediments that are present but the person is sacrificing those impediments—which means that he/she is not allowing those restrictions to dominate.

So, as we proceed with our training in esoteric studies or in spiritual science we are working on two fronts:

—Understanding of, and gaining appropriate control over, our personality;

—Understanding and working with Soul as the essence of our being.

This two-fold process assures us of steady spiritual development; it prepares us for discipleship and for membership in the New Group of World Servers, thus enabling us to serve humanity and the whole joyfully and lovingly through sacrifice, discipline and conscious awareness.

It must be emphasized that the *light* that one needs in order to understand self or reveal that which is hidden, comes from the Soul; the *love* that one needs to accept self and unite with the higher Self, comes from the Soul; the *power* that one needs to live courageously in accord with the truth of Self, comes from the Soul.

We might more accurately say that this light, love and power is in fact the Soul itself.

Transmutation, Transformation and Transfiguration

There are two broad, specific and distinct approaches to spiritual development work. Each has its place and time in every person's growth.

The first approach is *transmutation* which, in its more precise esoteric meaning, signifies any process used by the personality to change the personality for the better. This can include such self-chosen disciplines as physical exercise, balanced nutrition, emotional nurturing and mental concentration, all of which can be called 'character building.' It may also include psychotherapeutic processes and physical, emotional or mental therapies. While each may be used to treat a specific problem or body, they help to bring about an eventual integration of the bodies of the personality.

The goal (and limit) of transmutation is the harmonious integration of the personality so that it can be a more effective vehicle for Soul expression. When personal consciousness is centered in the personality, then transmutation processes need to be used. When the consciousness is more centered in the Soul than in the personality transmutation processes are not helpful; they are simply ineffective.

Until one is sufficiently Soul-infused one cannot adequately change the personality toward a greater state of union and harmony by using the Soul's energy directly. Until sufficient Soul-infusion takes place, the transmutational work of change must be done from the 'bottom-up' or from the 'outside-in'—that is, *by* the personality *on* the personality.

Transformation is the Soul-centered work of overcoming the remaining obstacles on the path of Soul-Personality union. Transformation is primarily directed at overcoming physical maya (inertia), emotional glamor (attachments) and mental illusions (distortions and misinterpretations of reality). The identification with the Soul's threefold energies (Will, Love and Light) and its application to the three respective levels (physical, emotional and mental) brings about the necessary changes. Although there are several different transformation techniques, transformation is essentially a conscious identification with Will, Love and Light, producing a conscious disidentification from maya, glamor and illusion. A change in being and attitude occurs naturally. The practice of transformation techniques is only useful once there has been a fundamental change in consciousness from form-identification to Soul-identification. The techniques are limited to maintaining this identification rather than causing it to come about. Whatever one's transformation practices, however, there is one which is absolutely essential—meditation. The primary purpose of meditation is to align the personality vehicles with the Soul, thereby enabling the Soul greater access to the form worlds in which its purpose and energies can be expressed.

Many people who aspire spiritually denigrate the transmutation processes and avoid the personality work necessary for further progress. Their spirituality is built on unstable ground and often vanishes in a crisis. Spirituality must never be a substitute for living in a challenging material world or for working with the personality with its limitations and problems. 'Spirituality' and 'materiality' are perceived as opposites, but each describes a greater or lesser degree of refinement of the continuum of life and consciousness. If either is denied, repudiated or feared, excess occurs in the opposite direction. Either excess is harmful and separative; the person is divided and an essential aspect of the whole is lost.

Some people try to solve their everyday problems by using some Soul techniques or Soul Light when they should simply be using their logic and reason. Personality tools should be used when they will do the job.

On the other hand, some people try to solve their health and economic problems with transmutational techniques such as visualization and affirmations, but to no avail. Their consciousness has become more Soul-centered and the old techniques no longer work for them. They now have to use a transformation process, the first of which is to discover the real, deeper reason why they have a problem. By discovering the meaning, they could go on to resolve the lack of alignment which is the cause. Similarly, when a transformation process needs to be used, a gestalt practice of intense emotional outpouring would be useless or harmful.

Many transmutational therapists and others centered in personality consciousness mistrust spirituality and the validity of transformation processes. Their mistrust is founded upon one or more factors:

a. They are afraid of the 'spiritual', perhaps because of associating it with 'religion' with which they have had some unpleasant or harmful experience;

b. They have observed the excesses of spirituality with the consequent harm that any excess can produce;

c. They have not seen useful or beneficial results from those who claim to use transformation processes;

d. They are unfamiliar with the whole level of transformation energies;

e. They feel threatened by a possible replacement for their own methods;

f. They do not know the limits of transmutation and assume that all they may ever need can be obtained through their transmutation methods;

g. They equate spirituality with mysticism and hold the view that Freud held, seeing mysticism as a form of "infantile regression."

h. They may be excessively materialistic;

i. They do not realize that psychological development is spiritual development.

By knowing the attainable goals and limitations of both transmutation and transformation we can all become more sensitive to their proper place and time in the quest for personal wholeness, and use whichever process will be most effective at any given time. Following the Law of Economy, which states that we must use the least amount of energy to fulfill a purpose, we must choose wisely.

There is a third approach to spirituality besides transmutation and transformation, but it is less of an approach than an attained state. It is called *Transfiguration*. Once transmutation has achieved its objective of overcoming mental illusion, it has produced such a large quantity of light that the individual transcends mental awareness and becomes intuitively aware of reality through identification with the Buddhic level. *The transcendence of the mental and the identification with the Buddhic Wisdom is Transfiguration.* The movement of consciousness involved has taken one from the human kingdom to the kingdom of Soul.

The Transformation Trinity

Three spiritual disciplines will assist one to bring Soul and Personality ever closer together. They are the trinity of Being or Unity viewed from a psychological-spiritual perspective. They are *obedience, discipline* and *sacrifice*—three of the most avoided practices by the personality ego because they are seen as antithetical to pleasure and personal comfort.

Obedience

Obedience trains the mind to grasp universal principles, archetypes and ideas and to think thoughts which accurately embody those ideas. Obedience is "potent in evoking the response of the two head centers to the impact of soul force, and unifying them into one field of soul recognition."[1] Through obedience to the higher, the mind becomes one-pointed and focused on the causal level. It can then function freely and powerfully and without frequent diversions from conditioning. 'To know the truth' becomes the motto of the obedient mind.

What one knows of the truth must be obeyed, otherwise the mind becomes split. 'Splitting the mind' is a form of mental suicide and can lead to a breakdown. A common way of splitting the mind is through lying. The truth must be told and lived for a person to have a healthy mind.

If something is true, it is true on all levels—"as above, so below" and vice versa. Anything that is true on one level has its correspondence on all other levels (the Law of Correspondences). If it does not, then it is not true; it is an illusion.

---

[1]Bailey, A.A., *Esoteric Psychology* II, 158.

Truth is self-evident, therefore it cannot or need not be proven. Truth originates from beyond the mind, so all the mind has to do is obey it and translate it into action—that is, live it. Who can perceive truth, or *the* truth of anything, is anyone who can see the evidence. There are varying degrees of mental clarity, however, and therefore there are a variety of responses to what is inherently self-evident.

There can never be any argument about what is true because either a person perceives the evidence or does not, or perceives a part of it while someone else may see a different part of it. For all practical purposes, therefore, truth is subjective—that is, what one *knows* of the truth is subjective. Any objectivity ascribed to truth is but a higher level awareness of some reality such as a Buddhic level idea. But even that is relative and subjective when one is aware on the Buddhic level and can sense higher levels. The only other 'objectivity' of truth is *consensual reality* where there is a consensus about something and a common agreement that something is as we say it is. But that is not true objectivity; it is a subjectivity shared with others.

The training of the mind is centered around the perception of the *truth of unity*, the oneness of being. Obedience requires the use of power to follow Divine Will rather than personal will.

> Serve and obey! These are the watchwords of the disciple's life. They have been distorted into terms of fanatical propaganda and have thus produced the formulas of philosophy and of religious theology; but these formulas do, at the same time, veil a truth. They have been presented to the consideration of man in terms of personality devotions and of obedience to Masters and leaders, instead of service of, and obedience to, the soul in all. The truth is, however, steadily emerging, and must inevitably triumph. Once the aspirant upon the Probationary Path has a vision of this (no matter how slight it may be), then the law of desire which has governed him for ages will slowly and surely give place to the Law of Repulse, which will, in time, free him from the thralldom of not-self. It will lead him to those discriminations and that dispassionate attitude which is the hallmark of the man who is on his way to liberation. Let us remember, however, that a discrimination which is based upon a determination to be free, and a dispassion which is the indication of a hard heart, will land the aspirant in the prison of a crystallized shell, which is far harder to break than the normal prison of the life of the average selfish man. This selfish spiritual desire is oft the

major sin of so-called esotericists and must be carefully avoided. Therefore, he who is wise will apply himself to serve and obey.[1]

Discipline

Discipline is the emotional or astral body's accurate response to the higher reality that the mind obeys. The mind sets the tone for elevated response by the astral body. This brings the lower reactive emotions from a level of self-centered preoccupation to a higher level of feeling in which devotion to an ideal becomes a dominant focus. The training of the emotions, directed by the mind, is to bring a feeling response to the *beauty of unity*, the oneness of being.

Beauty, like truth, is also highly subjective because its perception is directly related to a person's ability to touch the Soul where beauty exists. Beauty is the appearance of harmony wherein all aspects have a vital part in revealing the ultimate nature of Reality. Beauty is the heart of Life; it is Life as love. Beauty, therefore, can be only approached with the heart. The discipline of the emotions is to follow where the compassionate and loving heart leads. The destination is Unity.

Sacrifice

Beauty is the focus of the heart of love. It leads one to see the inherent *goodness of the one unified life* in every single expression and being. Sacrifice is the willing giving of oneself to this goodness, demonstrating the conviction that all is good, knowing that everything exists for good reason and serves the purpose of unity.

'Sacrifice' means 'making whole.' It involves training the body with its senses and active nature to let go of that which serves only the part (senses, appetites, the ego) and to actively choose and support that which serves the whole. Sacrifice is giving with the focus on goodness.

With sacrifice the body can act with light, with intelligence. The Light of the Soul infuses the brain, enabling it to see the inherent goodness in all people, all situations and all things, and then to think and act intelligently according to what it sees.

Obedience, discipline and sacrifice are the cornerstones of the integrated spiritual life. They are the means whereby Divine Will, Love and Light are brought into the transformation of the mental, astral and physical bodies. They open the door to Unity through the experience of its Truth, Beauty and Goodness.

---

[1]Bailey, A.A., *Esoteric Psychology*, Vol. II, 158-159.

When obedience, discipline and sacrifice are a way of living, then we *do* what we *know*, and we know what we *are*.

When we obey we resonate with the Atmic Plane. When we are disciplined we resonate with the Buddhic Plane. When we sacrifice we resonate with the Causal Body. When we live all three we are disciples and servers, expressing the essence of who we are.

CORRESPONDENCES

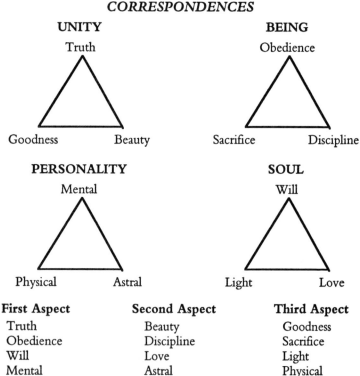

First Aspect	Second Aspect	Third Aspect
Truth	Beauty	Goodness
Obedience	Discipline	Sacrifice
Will	Love	Light
Mental	Astral	Physical

Truth is present whenever a universal law or principle is behind its expression or statement. Truth is relative to the degree it embodies the purity of the universal.

Beauty is present whenever something exists which is suited to fulfilling its purpose. Any function, action, situation or thing connected to its inherent purpose yields beauty.

Goodness is present whenever anything exists. Goodness is Godness; it is the third aspect of divinity. When anything manifests what it is, then we can say it is good, although ultimately everything is inherently good because it has the potential to manifest what it is by nature.

PART 2

THE HUMAN CONSTITUTION

VI

PERSONALITY

The personality is composed of three bodies:
—The mental body;
—The emotional or astral body;
—The physical body.

Until we know ourselves as Soul beings or Spiritual beings, we identify with our personalities, and believe that is who we are. We function as if we were our senses, our feelings and our thoughts. As stated in the Yoga Sutras of Patanjali, "The sense of personality is due to the identification of the knower with the instruments of knowledge."[1]

By experiencing life with our personalities and learning more about the true nature of our bodies, we will gain the ability and have the desire to disidentify from them, thus enhancing our freedom to use these bodies appropriately as vehicles of the Soul.

Tansley gives us a very beautiful and accurate description of the whole process of incarnation and the relationship of the personality to the rest of one's being. He writes:

> In order to incarnate, the Monad or Spiritual man appropriates six stable force centres: around these the subtle bodies are built. These force centres are known as permanent atoms, of which there are five, plus what is known as a mental unit. Permanent atoms are those atoms which have come under the attractive power of the second aspect of the Monad, the Son or Christ aspect.
>
> The ordinary atoms of our bodies are vitalized by the third or Mother aspect. These permanent atoms are the storehouses of karma, often spoken of as the 'Arbiters of Fate.' They are, if you like, data memory banks which determine the nature and quality of our bodies.
>
> Now the Will aspect of the Monad links with what is known as the Atmic Permanent atom. The Wisdom aspect links with the Buddhic Permanent atom and the third aspect of Intelligence or Mind links with

---

[1]Book II, 6.

82

what is called the Manasic Permanent atom. So the Monad expresses its first step towards incarnation through a triangle (of) energy.

The reaction of each of these three points of the triangle produces activity on what is called the higher mental plane, and this activity produces a force center or lotus which we call the soul. The soul consists of twelve petals surrounding a latent point of fire.

The soul, in order to penetrate deeper into matter, sounds its note, activating the permanent atoms of the low-self, and in deep meditation produces a thought-form which eventually precipitates upon the physical plane as a human being. Withdrawal of the soul's attention from this work of thought-form building results in a still birth.

A viable thought-form consists of a mental body, an astral or emotional body and an etheric body which is the archetype for the physical form.[1]

The Integrated Personality

The personality is more of a concept about the nature of the individuality than a true form. The individuality is basically of a selfish nature at first— and necessarily so. It expresses itself through the self-serving characteristics of each of the bodies of the lower self. There is no coordination or consideration of the other bodies when the focus is on one of them. For example, before the personality is integrated the individual will not consider the damaging effects of negative thinking on the physical body, or realize that emotional resentment toward another will erode personal feelings of self-worth.

Through expansion of consciousness, produced largely by suffering and perhaps some inspiration, there develops an increased mutual consideration on the part of the consciousness of each body. The selfish characteristics are seen to be a cause of suffering and are slowly transmuted into more accepting and loving qualities. Eventually these bodies begin to function as a single unit which we call an 'integrated personality'. You can imagine the increased power available to an individual who is integrated.

The integrated person generally has a stronger will than before, knowing what he or she wants and attracting the opportunities to carry out his or her will. There is the consciousness of being at the center of things but usually a sense of responsibility is also present. The individual's qualities become attractive forces, enabling one to serve more people more effectively.

---

[1]Tansley, D., *Radionics—Interface With the Ether-Fields*, 2-4. (C.W. Daniel Co. Ltd.)

The integration of personality proceeds by degrees. Initially the individual is quite self-centered, and could even be dedicated to evil, but eventually becomes more Soul-infused demonstrating idealism, compassion, service: able to sacrifice all for the sake of the whole.

The integrated personality who has a strong Soul influence is usually using the higher mental senses of discrimination and spiritual discernment, while the personality who is not so influenced by the Soul is using the force of the lower mind. In both cases the mind is the focal point of integration.

The magician must be an integrated personality, even when the magical powers are used for black magic. The 'black' magician does not have a strong Soul influence in the integrated personality, and so uses his powers for personal gain, manipulation and self-aggrandizement. The 'white' magician's mind is Soul illuminated, so he uses his power for the good of the whole.

VII

THE MENTAL BODY

Mind

The mental body is commonly called the mind, and most people's concept of the mind is closely linked with brain function. But mind is not limited to the brain. However, because the brain expresses aspects of the mind through its control of the physical body, through speech and through reasoning, the state of the mind tends to be judged by these brain functions. When there is impaired expression the person is often labeled 'mentally handicapped'. The lack of brain-mind coordination is neither an indicator of mental ability nor of mental impairment. The mind is a coherent field of energy, interpenetrating both the astral (emotional) body and the physical body with primary connections in the head centers of the body—hence its close association with the brain. Disorders in the etheric or dense physical bodies can result in a poor connection, giving the impression that the mind itself is somewhat lacking.

The word MAN is from the Sanskrit root, MANAS, which means THINKER. Mind is composed of manasic energy or substance. Man is, by definition, *the thinker*—one who cannot only know, but knows that he knows. This is self-consciousness; so MAN is a thinking, self-conscious being. This awareness can be present within or outside of a physical body, and can be present with an efficient brain as well as with a malfunctioning or diseased brain.

Everyone has a mind. It may be well developed or poorly developed. It may be active or merely a potential force awaiting activation—such as in primitive Man or in childhood. In modern Man the mind in general has been activated because of the present fifth root-race influence. However, most minds are still strongly influenced by emotions and desires. This type of mind is called 'Kama-manasic' in Sanskrit—a combination of astral and mental substance. With such a mind, conditioned as it is by emotions, there is a strong preoccupation with determining how to gratify one's desires. It is an egotistical, manipulative mind, constantly swayed by ever-changing emotional reactions. Such a

85

mind uses all of its activated powers to serve one's own will. It may not even know that there is a higher Will, much less seek to serve it.

Depending upon its stage of development, the mind:
—helps to preserve the identity of the lower self;
—acts as a way by which the higher Self can be known;
—serves as an intermediary between the Higher Self and lower self;
—functions as enlightened cause for all personality experiences.

The mental plane or body is customarily divided into two—the higher (abstract) mind and the lower (concrete) mind.

Higher Mind

The higher mind is the lower expression of the formless realms; that is why it is called 'abstract'. Through it one can contact the Planetary Mind and grasp some parts of the Plan which relate to his sphere of responsibility. It is the center of impersonal will and plays a significant role in helping the aspiring individual detach from personal will.

The intuition (Buddhic Plane) as pure love is represented in the higher mind as pure reason and pure light. The ideas of the Buddhic Plane are highly creative and magnetic ideas of Love. When the higher mind contacts these it is impressed with love's light in the 'formless form' of ideas, archetypes, symbols, principles and impulses. The activity of this light then begins intelligently to impress these abstract realities onto the lower mind so that they can be given a more specific, concrete form.

The higher mind's link with the lower mind is the Antahkarana or 'rainbow bridge' which is constructed through meditation, obedience, discipline, sacrifice, study and service.

Lower Mind

The lower mind is the highest aspect of the form worlds, just as the human is the culmination of the lower three kingdoms. It is the *reasoning principle*, the intelligence principle, projected into time and space. Since it is bound in time and space, reason proceeds in a linear fashion rather than following a simultaneous way of knowing, characteristic of higher intelligence. A trained mind will reason logically, perceiving the direct connections between one thing and another. Emotions are the enemy of logic because they are illogical and non-linear. A logical mind is a dispassionate, impersonal mind. If it is enlightened and impressed by the higher mind it can be extremely effective and creative. If it is not, it can be dangerously narrow, blind and destructive.

When the lower mind is linked with the higher mind its highest sense, *discrimination*, is activated. It can then distinguish between higher and lower, cause and effect, illusion and reality. Before the development of discrimination we can only guess, more or less well, about the meaning of things and the true nature of reality, caught as we are in illusion.

The lower mind is impressed from two directions—above and below. When it is open to higher impression it creates thought-forms (thoughts) which accurately portray some aspect of an ideal or principle. If there is mental stress or considerable influence from personality factors, the impressions from above will be distorted or misinterpreted, resulting in the creation of mental illusion. With the absence of discrimination one cannot tell that illusion has been created, and so merrily goes along acting as if the illusion were the reality. This blindness is true ignorance—that Gautama Buddha said was the fundamental cause of all suffering.

The lower influences on the mind come from:

—physical senses;
—emotions—active or repressed;
—past thoughts.

These produce a conditioned mind, inhibiting it to varying degrees from fresh insights and from life-enhancing creativity. Conditioning confines the mind to old patterns which keep repeating endlessly.

Mental Creativity

People seldom think a new thought. We rarely have original ideas. Observe your thoughts for an hour, and then extend this observation longer and longer. Besides developing your powers of observation, you will become familiar with the way your mind works, and will probably notice that virtually every thought you think is one you have thought before. The reason we keep repeating the past with our minds is because we have so much unfinished business which needs attention. There are incomplete relationships, feelings never expressed, plans never acted upon, dreams unfulfilled, desires left ungratified, aspirations abandoned, words not spoken, needs ignored. Everything seeks completion; that is natural. The past is constantly invading the present because the present is the only place where the past can be completed. So let us resolve to use the present constructively by thinking of ways to complete the various issues which come into our minds, and use the mind's willpower to act on them.

The higher mind perceives the world whole. The lower mind's role is that of analyst—seeing and understanding the parts more clearly which constitute the whole. As analyst it tries to answer the questions: who? what? where? when? how? The why?, however, can only be answered in relation to the whole, so it is answered by the higher mind.

The lower mind's temptation is to become too identified with and stuck in matter. This is the tendency toward inertia/maya. The antidote to arrest this stagnation is to challenge the mind to solve problems, to go further than it is accustomed to go, to learn new things, and to confront it with issues that can only be resolved by opening to the higher mind.

To function well mentally, the lower and higher minds need to be balanced:

—If too confined to concrete mental activity, engage in studies of a more abstract nature, such as philosophy and metaphysics;

—If too focused in abstract realms, engage in activities such as the natural sciences that require reason, logic and analysis.

There is an esoteric expression that many find confusing—*the Son of mind*. It means that Man, in his higher individuality, is an expression of the Universal or Divine Mind. It refers to the *intelligence principle* which is known by such names as Ego, Soul, Solar Angel or Christ Principle. It is more of a direct reference to the Buddhic Plane of ideas than to the mental plane. It refers to what Patanjali calls "the rain cloud of knowable things." It is the embodiment of the Divine Plan which the mind must grasp, translate and implement.

Lower mind, Son of Mind and higher mind are each capable of handling different dimensions of reality:[1]

Mind	Object	Realm	Worldview	Center
Lower Mind	facts	physical reality	belief or skepticism, opinion	throat
Son of Mind	truths	quality, values, aesthetics	faith	heart
Higher Mind	myth, truth	abstract, universal, transpersonal	knowledge	head/ crown

Developing Mind

There are many ways to develop the mind to make it more effective and efficient in doing what it is designed to do. These suggestions will serve to move the mind from inertia (tamas) to activity (rajas) and finally to rhythm (sattva).

---

[1] Cf. Sweigman, S. The Mental Plane. *The Beacon*, Sept-Oct 1983, 158 (Lucis Publishing Co.)

Inducing Altered States of Consciousness (ASC)

The normal waking state of mental reasoning and thinking produces beta brain wave activity which is 14 cycles per second and faster. This state of consciousness is considered normal for adults. *Normal* means it is the norm, the usual condition. The beta state is a stress-producing state which, to a degree, is necessary and useful. But when it is excessive it overloads the system and mental functioning is inhibited. Slower brain wave output needs to be encouraged for balance and stress release, so that the mind can function more clearly and efficiently. The rhythmic brain waves which are slower than beta are:

Alpha   7–14 cps.[1]
Theta   4–7 cps.
Delta   1/4–4 cps.

These are the altered states of consciousness (ASC). They are also normal in that they are all being produced all the time, but each one is characteristic of specific activities. For example:

Alpha—relaxation, daydreaming, concentration, rhythmic breathing, receptivity, loving, drug influence, hypnosis, sleep, meditation, play, listening to music or nature sounds, looking at beautiful objects, reading poetry, artistic activity, laughing, centering, turning inward, focusing on a seed thought, Soul activity.

Theta—sleep, deep hypnosis, intense creativity, dreaming, trance.

Delta—deep sleep, coma.

The alpha state is a highly desirable ASC because it is a state of assimilation and stress release. When there has been a preponderance of mental activity, the alpha state allows the mind to assimilate and integrate the input/output, thus reducing any potential overload and enabling it to proceed more effectively from the integrated level.

Follow some of the activities above for regularly inducing an ASC.

Relaxation

Relaxing the body gives the mind a greater ease in which to function through the brain and body. Any kind of relaxation produces an ASC. The increased stimulation of our senses and bodies in this modern world of complexity produces a great deal of stress. Relaxation does not happen automatically for us; we need to learn to relax until it becomes a natural response to our need for it and comes under the control of our will.

---

[1]cps = cycles per second

Visualization

In a relaxed state or ASC we can combine the mental capacity of thought-form-making with our astral body's sense of *imagination* to create images which will either:

—embody a higher mind reality, or

—create a positive feeling or model for right action.

Thus, we become effective as magicians and creators of our reality. We constantly create our feelings and experiences by the images we form. Unfortunately, many of these are unconsciously formed and projected and we are not aware that we have them. Many, too, are formed from a self-minimizing stance—worry, low self-esteem, denial, guilt, fear, etc. We can consciously create the feelings we want and the experiences we choose.

Images which give rise to negative, life-restricting feelings and experiences include:

- separation   - forcefulness
- isolation   - powerlessness
- incompetence   - inferiority
- victimization

Images which produce positive, life-enhancing feelings and experiences include:

- power (self-empowerment)   - ability
- competence   - unity
- beauty   - goodness
- love   - hope
- faith   - trust
- acceptance   - connectedness/relatedness
- ease   - sharing

and any of the Soul qualities previously mentioned.

Our fundamental nature is goodness and wholeness. This is the essential nature of Life. When we carry images that contradict goodness and wholeness we create a tension within ourselves, a friction between our true nature and our imagined nature. This friction produces a stress in our bodies. (Stress always stems from some fear.) We cannot experience stress when we are focused on a positive image.

When caught in a negative state there are various things one can choose to do:

—Imagine the opposite of what is felt;

—Disidentify from the feeling, and identify with your own being who *has* the feeling but *is not* the feeling;

—Form a symbol of what is being experienced (e.g., fear of death—symbol: coffin); then slowly change that symbol of fear into a symbol of love, of freedom, of happiness; then identify with the life-enhancing symbol;

—Enter into the negative so completely and fully that you actually go through it. This can work very well for physical pain, and with practicing detachment from desire. It can also work well for emotional and mental attachments;

—Have a 'homing thought'—an image of some idyllic place that is peaceful, harmonious, relaxing and joyful. It can be a place experienced outwardly or one created imaginatively. Use this image when needed.

Image Making

When visualizing or inducing relaxation, observe the following:

—Give complete and full attention to what is being done. This keeps you in the present moment where all power exists. Emotion and fear are rooted in the past or the imagined future. The present is a place of peace and courage; it is where the Soul is.

—Use as many of the senses as possible, or their inner counterparts. Feel, taste, hear, see and smell the various elements of the focus.

—Induce an ASC. This can be easily done with focused rhythmic breathing, single-pointed attention on something simple, music, a homing thought or progressive physical relaxation.

—Affirm in positive phrases what is inwardly being done or intended—e.g., "I am at peace," "My body is responding to my will with a deep feeling of ease," "I am filled with power and courage," "I am able now to experience harmony in my relationships," "I let go of the past struggling and flow easily through this situation."

Concentration

Concentration is the ability to focus the mind on whatever one chooses. It is voluntary attention. Usually we give attention involuntarily, the mind being attracted by stimuli rather than being directed by will. Being distracted is proof that mental discipline is lacking and that control of the mind needs to be developed. The effectiveness of mental direction and control is determined by the ability to hold the mind steady on the desired thoughts or activities. This increases the power to direct and create, to manifest personal will and to express Divine Will. Mental concentration is like physical exercise—the more one does, the greater the ability to use that body. Experiencing the mind through concentration is extremely simple—but not easy. It demands constant repetition and perseverance. Here is a developmental process you may wish to follow:

—Begin by keeping the attention on whatever the body is doing—if peeling potatoes, peel potatoes mentally; if driving a car, drive it with attention; if eating, eat with conscious awareness; if relaxing, relax with full mental presence. This voluntary attention goes by the name of 'mindfulness'—an important practice found in a Buddhist tradition, among others. (If concentration is not developed then it will be impossible to practice meditation, to focus on the true Self, or to "hold the mind steady in the Light"—an essential ability for true service.);

—When the mind is attracted to something, stay with it longer than you normally would, keeping your mind from wandering to associated thoughts which will progressively take you further and further away from the item of interest;

—Choose something which is not attractive or interesting to you and focus on it. Through willed attention you will learn to penetrate to its inner beauty, truth or goodness, and it may then hold your attention more readily;

—Practice willed concentration daily.

Concentration is not done by the mind, which is merely a body of energy. We concentrate the mental substance of this body, polarizing its atoms toward some object. But who does the concentrating? The individual entity does. And who is this entity? On the mental plane it is the will. The mental resonates with the Atmic and so contains the power of Will. Another way of understanding this is that the Soul is using the mental body in a disciplined way to express itself—its love, its understanding, its life. Concentration begins the life process of overcoming separation. Through concentration we begin to unite and become one with the objects of our concentration.

Many suggestions can be given to develop the will, but whatever disciplines one chooses must always have the objective of bringing personal will into alignment with Divine or Soul Will. If they do not do this and the personal will is strengthened separatively, all one ends up doing is increasing personal force. This is not will development. When force is increased there will be a consequent increase of resistance and suffering, a lack of clarity of purpose, and a diminished ability to express love.

Ways of developing will may include:

—Determining a proper sleeping schedule and sticking to it;
—Choosing physical exercises and doing them regularly;
—Avoiding 'junk food';
—Fasting;
—Refraining from immediate emotional reactions when someone says or does something you do not like;
—Listening attentively when someone is speaking to you (rather than thinking about what you are going to say next);
—Refraining from criticism, blame, jealousy, hatred and anger;
—Fulfilling your needs;
—Responding to the needs of others as you perceive them;
—Practicing tolerance and patience;
—Learning to control your speech through periods of silence;
—Making an effort to express your thoughts clearly in the most accurate language;
—Composing rules for self-improvement and adhering to them;
—Keeping your workspace and living space clean and tidy;
—Reciting the Great Invocation or other prayers or mantras daily;
—Being punctual;
—Keeping your word and following through on your promises and commitments.

Meditation

In light of mental development, meditation is a vital key to aligning the lower mind with the higher mind. It is a necessary means of building that lighted bridge called the Antahkarana. Through meditation we can access the power to mentally create loving realities which produce harmony and elevation. The meditative focus must be some reality greater than the self-interest of the individual. The focus is to be on a Soul quality which will be universal.

Clear Verbal Expression

Clear thinking is enhanced by clear verbal expression. Getting the right words matched to the thoughts is an important part of linking the brain to the mind. An effort must be made to bring the two together. Some people think clearly but do not pay attention to how those thoughts are expressed. Words are carelessly chosen or unconsciously used, and allowed to come out automatically. The result is poor communication and a clouding of the thoughts. What begins as clear thinking may end up as confused chatter.

When we focus on clear expression we may come to the realization that our thoughts are often not clear. We should learn to be silent when that happens or use the opportunity to clarify our thinking.

Since it is not possible to have a clear concept without a word for that concept, increasing one's vocabulary is a useful way of expanding conceptual thinking. It also gives one a greater versatility, power and effectiveness in expressing clearly more difficult or abstract thoughts. With a broad range of words at one's command, the right word can be chosen to produce the effect one intends. The white magician is as adept at wielding the power of the word as he is at creating powerful and appropriate thought-forms.

Broadening The Mind

There are many beneficial ways to broaden one's knowledge, sensitivity, awareness and skills which relate to mental development. A few could be mentioned, such as:

—Participating in different types of cultural activities—recreational, artistic, literary, cinematic, culinary, social, business, etc;
—Studying other cultures and civilizations;
—Visiting other countries and experiencing their people, environment and culture;
—Learning another language;
—Expressing oneself in some unknown field, unrelated to what one usually spends time doing—e.g., learning to operate or program a computer, playing a musical instrument, or taking a course in public speaking;
—Reading widely, touching upon several different fields of human activity and human interests;
—Keeping up-to-date on world events, learning to see relationships between various events and discovering why they are happening.
—Studying psychology—orthodox and esoteric.

VIII

THE ASTRAL BODY

The Plane of Duality

A Master of Wisdom has said that the astral plane is a creation of Man. From an esoteric point of view this may be totally true. From the angle of experience it unquestionably is. The word 'astral,' which means 'of the stars', has traditionally been used to refer imprecisely and generally to the 'higher planes'—that is, to all those that are higher than the physical. In more precise esoteric terminology it refers to the plane of desire and reaction which, in our human constitution, is the emotional body. Its 'starry' meaning may refer to the usually bright, changeable, colorful nature of the astral. In fact, viewed clairvoyantly, the landscape of the astral plane itself is much brighter than its physical counterparts. Thought-forms which are clothed in astral substance are very definite and colorful, although if the thoughts and feelings are vague, the astral forms will also be vague. Colors and sounds are often more distinctive and rich. The life of its natural elements—trees, flowers, animals etc.—appear to be much more alive and vital.

Not everyone agrees with this description. Some describe it as filled with confusion and chaos, very nebulous with barely discernible forms. Perhaps the discrepancy is due to the level of the astral being described.

In general, the lower astral subplanes are hell and the higher subplanes are quite heavenly. Because of the former we are usually taught by spiritual and esoteric teachers to detach ourselves from the astral and to stand free from its influences. But it is a plane of our existence, just as are the physical and mental planes. Each has its purpose, each must be experienced, and when we have learned what we need to learn in each we must let them go. By detaching ourselves from them we can then use them when and how it is beneficial to express our true Divine Self in matter. We cannot control that to which we are attached. Control can only be attained with sufficient familiarity with a substance, which comes through experiencing it directly, and with detachment from it.

The astral body of humanity is a very potent influence in the world today. Not only is it replete with simple human desires, but since the development of the lower mind has progressed so significantly, the desire nature has been intensified by mental power and direction. Everyone on this earth is affected by and contributes to humanity's astral body. Everyone is working to some degree in astral matter, either being controlled by it or learning to use it as a vehicle for expressing Love.

The astral plane resonates with the Buddhic plane and is potentially a fertile field in which the unity of love can be learned. But unity cannot be expressed until separatism and duality are known. Love on the astral plane is therefore experienced selfishly at first (getting love, being loved), and then as a resolution or harmony of duality in relationships.

Duality is a primary characteristic of the astral plane. The realm of opposites exists here because of:

—the lower mind's nature of separating reality into parts;
—the emotional experience of pain and pleasure;
—the physical survival instinct to separate oneself from, and to protect oneself from, threats—real or imaginary;
—the law of attraction and repulsion.

Duality is a necessary and natural outcome of the polarity between the unmanifest and the manifest, spirit and matter. Through the experience of duality the true nature of spirit and matter are discovered and the mental faculty of discrimination develops as a vital tool for redemption and integration—eventually leading to oneness, or unity of matter and spirit.

All energy is essentially spirit. As spirit manifests itself, intelligence responds. This response is a reaction from the opposite polarity of spirit. The reaction awakens desire, or desire is the result of the reaction, or desire is the reaction to the presence of spirit. Desire is an astral body reflection of the Will of life. Desire, therefore, is the impulse toward unity or fusion with all life. This impulse is behind every desire, no matter how base the desire appears to be. The result of this process is the creation of Soul, and of Soul consciousness. Hence, through desire we come to know ourselves as Soul. Desire ceases when there is no longer the feeling of separation or lack.

Soul plus personality response to Soul creates the astral. This interaction and striving for fusion produces desire and the whole astral dimension. In this astral we experience heaven (Soul) and hell (separate individual nature). Through the resolution of this duality, personality first forms, followed by Soul infusion.

The whole crux of the astral is in its duality. Desire pushes the duality experience to the extreme. When sufficient duality is experienced, the experience begins to produce discrimination based on the pain/pleasure principle. Pleasure is chosen over pain and eventually leads to happiness and joy which is achieved through Christ consciousness or ascension to the Buddhic plane.

The astral dimension is the human realm wherein good and evil are first experienced. This is the duality based on pain/pleasure or attraction/repulsion. Religion, which is the traditional spiritual path associated with the astral, sets up concepts, rules and characteristics about God and the devil. These have become culturally ingrained in our collective psyche to represent the ultimate duality, so much so that it is very difficult to follow one's inner path without being obstructed by this conditioning. The difficulty with these concepts is that they are perceived to be absolutes and therefore inhibit the ability to transcend psychically the duality that they represent and to experience the unity or synthesis of the opposites.

From another perspective, the astral dimension can be seen to be all our attachments and projections resulting from mental perceptions. Thought impresses itself in astral matter because a fundamental characteristic of astral substance is its highly sensitive impressionability. These mental perceptions might be of truth or of illusion. Both are equally impressed within the astral body. As these perceptions are received by the emotional body, or as we react to the perceptions with our feelings, the result is the astral dimension. So we can say that the astral is the reactive level of consciousness to thought, subconscious elements, Soul, Spirit, etc. A reaction always exists to the degree that there is or is not fusion or unity between the astral body and the Soul. The greater the unity the less the reaction. Reaction is a form of opposition or resistance. The resistance is due to pushing away that which is not perceived as self (ego). The Soul, because of its persistent presence, progressively influences the astral body and the reactions diminish. With the lessening of emotional reaction the emotional body becomes more pure in the sense that it is now able to reflect and mirror higher reality more accurately. It becomes a vehicle of the intuitive or buddhic plane through which love is able to be expressed with minimal selfishness. The perfected astral body is but a lower reflection of the intuitive realm. Reaction is due to:

Ignorance—The lower mind does not yet know that the influences it is experiencing are coming from the Soul and have the noble purpose of leading the separated ego back to unity with the higher Ego;

Fear—The astral substance is coalesced around the survival instinct of the separated self, and feels that the love which the Soul is projecting through all experience is a threat to the ego's survival.

Reaction ceases when ignorance and fear are overcome. By discovering meaning in all experience the mind *knows*, and by detaching from the ego the astral body *loves*. *Reaction* is then replaced with appropriate *response* to all experience. Such response is always intelligent, enlightened love.

Desire

Behind every emotion is a desire. If the emotion is 'negative'—such as fear, anger, hatred or jealousy—there is an unfulfilled desire, or what we call a selfish desire (wanting to get something for oneself, without necessarily having relationship to real need). When the emotion is 'positive'—such as happiness, excitement, praise or gratitude—there is a fulfilled desire which then overflows in a rushing out of energy to give to another. Fulfilled desire eventually leads to aspiration—a yearning for and a giving to union with 'the other', and within that, the 'ultimate Other', the Divine.

The greatest sin is denial. To deny desire is to repress the urge which can eventually lead to union with Divine Will. Desire is a force enkindled by Divine Love in form. Denial is an act of pushing this force into unconsciousness from where, in the subconscious, it will continue to exert itself because the nature of Love is consciousness. It will seek acceptance and consciousness. When anything is denied or repressed into the subconscious, its influence, as it struggles to be released into the light of awareness, is always negative. *Negative* can be equated with unconsciousness. It can produce such effects as poor self image, authoritarianism, feelings of unworthiness, anger, frustration and criticism.

Sin

Sin means to 'miss the mark'. It is inappropriate action, without moral implications. It is caused by ignorance and fear and can be overcome through development of consciousness. Punishment is an inappropriate response to sin. Punishment lacks intelligent and loving understanding of what sin is. Because sin misses the mark of truth and is a result of not knowing the truth, or knowing it and being shackled by fear of responding to it, there will be natural consequences, often unpleasant and painful. The law of cause and effect prevails and the 'sinner' learns in time to hit the mark, if only to avoid the unpleasant consequences. Punishment for sin is inherent within the act. This is nature's way of keeping us on track.

Feelings, urges, impulses and desires—however 'bad' or 'good' they are judged to be—are valid. They exist for a reason and must be accepted and owned. We must take responsibility for them because we have, at some level, created them. They are a result of previous thought and action, or a result of Soul influence. In either case they are a means for further progress and eventual perfection. They are opportunities for growth even when they appear powerfully negative. Acceptance does not mean expression. For example, if you are feeling angry, accept your anger as a valid feeling rather than denying that you are angry. If you repress the anger it will continue to burn and boil in the subconscious and may produce some unpleasant effects such as ulcers, resentment or sharp words when not called for. Once you have accepted your anger try to get at the root of it; find out why you are angry. You will discover an unfulfilled desire or expectation, and behind that will be found some type of fear. So instead of expressing your anger in angry words and actions, which will inevitably hurt someone or something, expend the emotional energy in action which fulfills the desire and conquers the fear.

You may, on the other hand, choose to suppress the anger. Unlike repression, which is denial, suppression involves acceptance followed by a temporary suspension. Suppression is a conscious choice to deal with the issue at a later time or in another way. If you don't feel willing or able to adequately deal with it at the moment you may put it on hold until you are ready. If you have sufficient Soul power, you may choose to deal with the issue from that level. In psychology this is called *sublimation of feelings*.

Avoid denial. Be aware of your desires. Conscious desires are transmutable; unconscious desires are not. We can become aware of what is unconsciously desired (often called 'personal needs')—e.g., the desire to be loved, when unconscious, can lead to subtle manipulative behavior. These unconscious desires motivate us to do many things. We can learn what they are by observing our behavior, as our actions frequently arise from the subconscious. Since these desires are part of the subconscious, and the subconscious is closely connected with the physical body, these desires are anchored in the physical body. So by feeling the body and getting into closer attunement with it, we can discover these desires which come from conditioning, fears, aspirations, perceptions, feelings of limitations, feelings of expansion, and so forth.

Do not deny desire. Accept whatever the desire is. When you know it you can transmute it or express it. If you are attuned to the Soul, the purpose of the desire is seen and it can then be expressed appropriately.

Desire is the power for purpose (Will). It leads one to the highest astral sense (emotional idealism) which, when developed, is able to be expressed as union with the Divine. This is possible only when the lower mental senses, especially discrimination, have been developed. By working consciously with our desires and the world of duality in which we find them we will develop discrimination.

Fear

Behind every desire is a fear. Fear is separation. Its opposite is love or oneness. Fear arose through the creative process when *involution* occurred—when the monadic spark of the Divine descended into matter and assumed a separate identity as a conscious human being. Through simple consciousness—before self-consciousness was present—there was the feeling of isolation and separation from the Divine Source. As self-consciousness develops, evolution begins and the individual recognizes that he only *appears* to be separate, that the Divine is within Its creation and in every part of it. With this awareness Love is born within the heart, conquering fear. Fear is transmuted into Love and "death shall be no more."

Fear is fundamentally the fear of death—death representing any form of lack or loss. Every desire is ultimately a desire for Love. Every desire, motivated by fear, is an attempt to overcome death by obtaining what we feel is lacking and by holding onto what we are afraid of losing.

The irony of life is that we lack nothing and can lose nothing. If our consciousness is focused on material levels we obviously do not possess everything and what we do possess can be lost. But this materialistic world is a world of illusion. What we possess makes little difference to how we are in our true being and has little meaning in relation to the deep fulfillment for which we yearn. Possessions have only secondary relevance to our true needs. When we wake up to who we really are we realize that we lack nothing. We are the fullness of all abundance; we have all the power, love and light that we could ever dream of having. The fact that we are so materialistic makes it difficult for us to see what we are because we only see what we have expressed outwardly of this power, love and light.

Our one fundamental need as Soul beings in bodies is the need to express love. (The bodies respond to this in its shadow form as the need to be loved.) Since our Soul nature is essentially Love, and we have three vehicles suitably adapted to the three lower worlds in which Love needs to be expressed, we lack no opportunity to fulfill our basic need. If we feel unfulfilled it is not because of any real lack, but because we choose to try to *get* love rather than to *express* love. And we do this only because we are not aware of who we are, wanting to hang on to the illusory identity of the separated self.

Sacrificing ego identity is a way of learning to accept the Self and express love. The Law of Sacrifice is the law of 'those who choose to die'. Sacrifice overcomes the fear of loss because it is a willing choice of the whole, the Soul, the one Self. Dying consciously is letting go of the small, narrow life to enter into "life more abundant." Through sacrifice, one moves from the illusion of not *having all* to the realization of *being all*. Being simply *is*. With the consciousness of being there is no separation and therefore no loss. We cannot lose what we are.

We can truthfully say, when we know the truth in our hearts and bodies, "I lack nothing of value, I can lose nothing of value. I am and have, for all eternity, all there is."

Feelings

Feelings, in an esoteric sense, are somewhat distinct from emotions, but both relate to the astral body. Feelings are of finer quality than emotions. Feelings may be said to be astral responses to higher values and levels, while emotions could be considered to be astral reactions or impressions from the world of form and the lower levels of reality. As various influences and stimuli reach the astral body, feelings and emotions result.

Astral Body	Source of Influence	Astral Result
Lower subplanes	Physical body, senses, physical world Subconscious Lower mind	Reaction/Emotion/Desire/"Self."
Higher subplanes	Intuition (Buddhic Plane) Higher Mind (Soul)	Response/Feeling/Aspiration/"Other."

The lower subplanes of the astral are influenced by Light, but because of the opaqueness of these levels, more shadow than light is present. Hence, blindness, darkness and distortion are typical. The higher subplanes are influenced predominantly by Love; hence, their outgoing propensities. Our objective is to increase awareness on the higher subplanes and then use the lower subplanes to express that awareness. The basic orientation

of the higher subplanes will be one of devotion and emotional idealism—
a giving of one's love to support, and to identify with, a higher object or
being of Beauty. The use of the imagination (an astral body sense) is
useful in supporting such an orientation to Beauty.

Astral Stimulants

The astral body can be stimulated by virtually anything, but there are
some things that have a greater resonance on the astral level than on other
levels:

—Alcohol;

—Many drugs including marijuana, but excluding tobacco which
resonates on etheric levels;

—Most television programs and movies which appeal to the emotions
as their entertainment value. These would have elements of
romance, love and hate, horror, violence, sex, good vs. evil, power,
struggle;

—Anything with a strong emphasis on duality which elicits reaction
on one or the other side of an issue;

—Most popular music, including rock music, country and western and
even ballads;

—Religious music and devotional hymns;

—National anthems;

—Much of the 'news' selected for broadcast and print in the media.

—Many popular magazines, especially the popular tabloids;

—Food which appeals to the appetite rather than to hunger. Such
foods often emphasize sweetness and saltiness (extreme yin or yang).
When a person is out of balance (i.e., yin or yang is too strong)
food often becomes an emotional compensation for the restoration
of the needed balance;

—Religion in general, but especially fundamentalist religion;

—Gossip and provocative speech.

Some teachers speak about intensifying the astral body. This
intensification creates a variety of imbalances from excessive stimulation
to possibilities of extreme rigidity. Means of intensification can include:
certain breathing exercises, specific Hatha yoga postures, some mantras,
excessive Tai Chi, sexual activity, some drugs and music such as heavy
metal and rock.

The more a person is exposed to influences such as these, particularly if
the experience is strong (e.g., more than one or two alcoholic drinks,
enough drugs to alter perception, several hours of television, etc.) the

more one's astral body will be stimulated. In that stimulation or shaking, without the purposeful guidance or direction from the mind, there can be released a variety of latent emotions—emotions that may be connected with past experiences either from this life or from other lives. What often also happens is that when the stimulation is a result of mass media influence, the emotions of humanity's astral body can be experienced, and one is taken into greater identification with the masses. Much of the astral vibration is lower level negativity and will tend to draw out the negative emotions. The more sensitive a person is, the truer this will be. Sensitivity reflects the ability to attune, to be at-one-with. Through emotional identification which is the result of such stimulation, a person loses himself.

Exercises in Control

Some suggestions for controlling emotional response to entertainment and influences with which one is in constant contact may be helpful:

—The easiest way of controlling emotional response is through simple avoidance of those influences that are not necessary or beneficial.

—Minimize exposure to potentially harmful influences.

—Exercise a sense of detachment. For example:

- watch a movie all the way through to a few minutes before the conclusion and then go on to something else;
- decide to buy a treat (something unnecessary), enjoy the idea of having it, and then change your mind not to do so.

For such responses as the above, when the mind is changed from the original intention it should be done in favor of some superior or alternate personal value so that the new movement does not become a denial causing frustration but a choice for something greater in which any potential frustration is sublimated.

—Maintain a sense of attunement to the Higher Self so that a proper perspective may be maintained and higher emotional energies such as tolerance and compassion may prevail.

Astral Remedies

When the astral body is disturbed and no longer responsive to higher ideals and thoughts a variety of negative emotional states are experienced including irritation, depression, frustration, impatience, fear, anger, guilt, etc. There is a lack of feeling good and an inability to feel and express love in meaningful ways.

There are a variety of things a person can do to remedy emotional disturbances. The following are some suggestions:

Inner Direction

Use the mind to think desirable and pleasing thoughts. The astral disturbance is caused by disturbing thoughts, so the mind has to take a different direction.

Discover what you really value, and work to express those values. For example, if you value meditation then meditate; if you value a healthy body, then exercise it, feed it nutritionally, and give it enough rest. Disturbance occurs when one is experiencing a devaluation of one's ideals, principles and values.

Focus on a meaningful challenge—something which will require effort and courage to master, and will result in a good sense of self and a feeling of accomplishment.

Practice detachment from emotional reactions—i.e., allow the reactions to occur, but do not identify with them. Remain the observer.

Identify with the true Self rather than the reacting self. View influences from the perspective of the Soul in order to be able to maintain a balanced understanding and a sense of power.

Remain in a giving, loving, helping attitude so there can be response rather than reaction. Response is other-directed; reaction is self-centered.

Every negative influence is but a distortion, misinterpretation, lack or excess of a positive reality. Discover the hidden positive reality and relate to it, thereby developing discrimination.

Ask yourself the question: "What can I learn from this situation?" Explore possibilities for growth.

Every negative is a part of a whole. Ask yourself, "What is the whole picture of which this is but a part?" The whole picture will be a positive, growth promoting reality.

A negative emotion is based on an illusion resulting from a distortion, misrepresentation or misinterpretation of truth. This truth is an ideal. Search for the ideal and direct your feelings toward it in a devotional way.

Pray to the inner God or Guide of your being. Use invocation, such as *The Great Invocation* or *Mantram of Unification*.

Aspire to something greater.

Use the imagination to create life-enhancing images.

Outer Treatment

Some methods use things or substances that can help restore balance to the emotional body. They can be used as adjuncts to the inner direction or to get the processes moving in the direction of the inner in extreme situations.

Radionics. When the exact situation has been assessed, the appropriate vibrational antidote can be broadcast. If, for example, depression has set in, the vibration of joy can be sent to elevate the astral atoms to a higher orientation.

Flower Essences. The traditional Bach flower remedies, the California flower essences, and others following the same principles of preparation, are most effective on astral levels.

The primary center of the astral body is the solar plexus, and according to David Tansley[1] all the Bach remedies work through the solar plexus chakra, but on three different levels. The following, he says, work on the mental level: agrimony, cerato, cherry plum, gentian, olive, scleranthus and hornbeam. Rockwater was said to work on the etheric level, while all remaining remedies work on the astral level.

Complete directories for the use of flower essences can be obtained where the remedies are available. Consider the following applications:

Oak: For the depression suffered by those people who fight against adverse conditions without loosing hope.

Gorse: For deep hopelessness.

Mimulus: For the known fears of everyday life such as fear of people, animals, the dark, etc.

Rock Rose: For extreme fear, terror and panic.

Wild Oat: Dissatisfaction and uncertainty.

Centaury: For those who lack the willpower to refuse the demands of others.

Impatience: For impatience and irritability.

Chicory: For those who are possessive and over-critical of others.

Heather: For the talkative, self-absorbed people who fear loneliness.

Gentian: For doubt and discouragement.

Red Chestnut: For fear and over-anxiety for others.

Aspen: For vague fears of unknown origins.

Chestnut Bud: For those who are slow to learn even from repeated experiences.

---

[1] cf. Tansley, D., *Radionics and the Subtle Anatomy of Man*, 88-89. (C.W. Daniel Co. Ltd.)

Larch: For those who lack confidence in themselves and have the fear of failure.

Star of Bethlehem: For shock.

Holly: For those who suffer from feelings of envy, jealousy, revenge and suspicion.

Willow: For resentfulness and bitterness.

Pine: For self-reproach.

Mustard: For deep depression and gloom.

Gem Remedies. These can be taken orally as a gem-potentized solution or pilules, or the gems themselves can be used directly on the body. The advantage of the potentized remedies is that two or more can be easily combined. Dr. A. Bhattacharya, who has written books on the subject, uses them extensively at his clinic in Naihati, India. Gem therapy is not only effective for astral body disturbances, but is equally useful for treating the mental body as well as physical body diseases.

Homeopathy. While homeopathic treatment is most frequently associated with physical conditions, there are homeopathic remedies also suited to treating the astral body, especially in situations where there is a disturbance in the astral-etheric-physical connections such as frequently exist in the endocrine glands and nervous system.

Color. Particularly resonant on the astral plane, color therapy can be quite beneficial when used externally such as with colored lights, clothing, and decoration, or when taken internally as potentized remedies. The twelve-color system developed by Dinshah is one of the best systems.

Physical Treatment. Very often there is either a congestion or a lassitude in the astral body due to lack of physical expression of the feelings. A simple physical treatment might involve physical exercise in the form of walking, working or dance. A more specific treatment might revolve around correcting hormonal imbalances or toning the nervous system.

Sound. Appropriate sounds for specific conditions can be intoned or made with musical instruments, which is the practice in sound therapy and music therapy. The more common practice is simply to expose the subject to suitable pre-recorded music which has been determined to produce the desired changes. In general, any kind of uplifting music will prove beneficial to harmonizing and raising the vibrations of the astral body. Much of the so-called 'New Age' music has this effect.

Art Therapy. Experiencing a renewed popularity, art therapy can be very helpful in exposing emotional problems and working through a healing process.

Psychotherapy. A variety of techniques are used. When most effective, they bring the astral body into harmony with both the lower and higher mind, enabling the individual to feel the power of Love deep within and to express it more freely through the emotional body.

Regardless of the techniques used to bring about a renewed harmonious vitality in one's emotional life, the ultimate objective must always be to gain control of the emotions so that the astral body becomes a clear vehicle for expressing the Soul's love nature in response to need. Anything short of this is incomplete, necessitating further disturbance to force the consciousness to expand further until the goal has been reached.

Astral Projection

There is quite a fascination with astral projection, or 'astral travel' as some call it, when an individual is beginning to take an interest in inner realities. It is a type of detachment from the physical body in which one can experience realities of the astral plane. It is a practice fraught with all kinds of traps and problems and should, as a deliberate exploration, be avoided. When we have sufficient mastery of our own emotions we will be able to work and serve consciously on the astral plane. Until then it is sufficient to encounter the astral plane in our sleep, which we often do not recall in waking consciousness because of a lack of registration in the brain. Sometimes, however, an experience can be recalled when the brain is impressed. Often the mood that prevails upon awakening is a direct result of our astral experience in sleep.

Out-of-body experiences (O.O.B.E.s) can and do happen automatically under anesthesia, during severe danger or a life-threatening situation, in intense aspiration, meditation and contemplation, as well as during sleep. These present no real danger, with the possible exception of a drug-induced O.O.B.E. In these cases, one must first consciously direct the feeling nature and the mind to focus on a high level reality without the presence of any fear. It is important that those in attendance when a person is anesthetized refrain from negative comment. In fact, it is best that they be silent because whatever is said will be impressed upon the patient's astral body and become a part of the subconscious.

Accidents in which a person loses consciousness may cause the same condition as does anesthesia. Great care must be taken to place the victim in a comfortable position and maintain silence until consciousness returns.

Conscious withdrawing from the physical body is practiced by those people sufficiently evolved to do so for selfless reasons such as rendering a particular service. These people are initiates; they have practiced daily meditation for many years; they have a strong nervous system and a healthy body. They know how to function on the subtle planes and they know the laws of these inner realms.

The Astral World

The astral plane is a world of such tremendous diversity that it is almost impossible to describe briefly.[1] Because the astral realms can be perceived by quite a number of psychically sensitive people of varying degrees of development, we have numerous and varied accounts of the nature of the astral world.

Observations on the astral plane can also easily be distorted because many of its inhabitants have the ability to change their forms very quickly and to cast a glamor over the undeveloped psychic.

Astral vision has another peculiarity in that objects appear in a whole kind of way, revealing not only their outer form but also their inner reality. Because of this it is common to confuse a number that is seen on the astral level. For example, 321 can easily be mistaken for 123. The observer has to learn not only to see correctly but also to translate accurately what is seen. There is a principle that operates in all planes and in the bodies of these planes possessed by the human being: that each plane is composed of seven subdivisions, each of which is either higher or lower—that is, faster or slower in vibration—than the others. With reference to human bodies, this means that the lowest or slowest vibratory level is closest to the dense physical body. That which is higher or faster in vibration extends further away from the physical body. This means, for example, that the astral body interpenetrates the etheric-physical body and part of it extends beyond the confines of the physical body, giving the impression of being outside the physical body. This extension, which is often very colorful, is what is usually perceived to be the *aura*. In the astral plane itself it follows that there are a great range of qualities and beings relating to each of the seven subdivisions of the plane. The astral subplanes do not exist one on top of the other any more than they do within the astral body but simply exist as interpenetrating levels of qualities, totally present wherever the physical is present. This means that the astral plane exists here where the earth exists and where humanity exists. However, inhabitants of the astral plane are usually only conscious of their own plane; the earth and the physical world are invisible to them.

---

[1] C. W. Leadbetter in his book, *The Astral Plane*, describes much of the astral world in a very understandable way.

The seventh, or lowest, subdivision of the astral plane is what we referred to earlier as *hell*. All that is light and good and beautiful seems invisible when on this plane. The darkness and cruelty often experienced here radiate from within the entity and cause its existence to be of a negative quality. This subplane lies partly on the surface of the earth and partly—perhaps mostly—*beneath* the surface. The average decent human doesn't normally experience this region and is often not conscious of it.

On the higher subplanes, the 'spirits' create—temporarily—things familiar to them: houses, schools, cities, hospitals, landscapes, etc. These 'people' go to school, cook meals, eat, smoke, play music, go to hospitals and do all the things that were habitual while in physical incarnation.

There are astral records that are often referred to as Akashic Records. In fact they exist at the higher mental level as part of the causal body of the Soul, be it individual or the Soul of the world. Anyone who claims to be able to read the Akashic Records is invariably reading but their impression in astral matter, rather than in their authentic light within the higher mental plane. The reading of them will therefore be distorted because of the distortions that occur when the impressions are created in astral substance.

Leadbeater makes reference to a variety of inhabitants in the astral dimension and describes them in various categories.[1]

> The astral dimension is frequented by people who are alive in physical bodies, by adepts in their 'mayavirupa' (temporary body of illusion), and by humans who no longer have physical bodies—the ones referred to as 'dead'.
>
> After physical death everyone passes through the astral dimension, remaining there anywhere from a few days to a few centuries. The unselfish and spiritually oriented will often move more quickly through this realm than the person who lived a self-serving or harmful life. The real determinant is the amount of astral matter found in one's astral body created by the quality of life lived, by the emotional tenor of the personality and by the desires one has indulged.
>
> When all is said and done we must realize that as a dimension of existence the astral is a temporary state, one in which we do not as a rule find enlightened beings.

---

[1] Cf. Leadbeater, C.W., *The Astral Plane*. (The Theosophical Publishing House)

IX

PSYCHISM AND CHANNELING

Psychism

Psychism is an expression of the Soul and refers simply to the activation of any of the non-physical senses, most notably those of the astral and mental bodies. It is the energy of consciousness unfolding in the human context and is relative to the degree of unfoldment of individual awareness. When there is awareness through the astral and lower mental senses we say there is *lower psychism*. When awareness is on the higher mental levels—or even on intuitive levels—we say there is *higher psychism*. Either of these two levels of psychism can be used with impunity, but when the powers of the senses are used with selfish motive against the true nature of the Soul and the evolutionary Plan, we have *distorted psychism* which requires remediation.

Distorted psychism usually begins in lower psychism and stems from the desires, illusions, glamors, and vanities found particularly in the astral body. The distortion is unintentional and the one in whom it exists is unaware of the distortion. At times there is imposition of will, psychological projection, manipulation of others or various manifestations of selfishness. Black magic is an extreme example of distorted psychism.

Lower psychism (the development and expression of the lower senses) should never be desired, but if it manifests it should be accepted as natural. Some people are born with clairvoyance and clairaudience and these must be accepted as natural. They are usually a result of previous development. These powers and others will naturally develop as one progresses on the spiritual path when the Soul makes its influence more strongly felt in the astral and lower mental bodies. Their presence then also needs to be accepted as natural, but must never be relied upon for guiding others until the higher mental senses—notably *discrimination* and *spiritual discernment*—are developed. Until the higher are developed there is no ability to tell when impressions are accurate, when it is right to share them, or what effect the divulging of them will have on others.

In lower psychism there may be a genuine and accurate inner contact made, but because it is made by one who is colored by his own desires and glamors, there will be a distortion. Desires and attachments remain in the astral body as filters through which all astral activity passes, giving it a highly personal tone. For example, if a client asks a lower psychic if she is going to travel the psychic may respond, "Yes, you are going to China." The psychic who has a strong desire to go to China, may have accurately sensed the 'travel vibration' or travel desire in the client and then unconsciously combined that impression with his own desire, producing the statement given. This is not uncommon practice. Most psychics today who 'read' for others operate in the cloudy sphere of lower psychism.

Many people desire to be in contact with a spirit guide or some great being of wisdom. The *belief* that this is possible along with the *desire* creates a picture in their astral body. Subsequently any impression that comes from a higher source passes through that image giving the impression that the *image* is the source of the information. Likewise, any impression which is not consciously received may be attributed to the same source, when it could simply be surfacing from the subconscious. Without discrimination and discernment such self-delusion is common.

Desires, particularly repressed desires, can give rise to the formation of sub-personalities with 'voices'. When there is a pattern of unfulfilled desires and of avoidance of meeting one's true needs, the sub-personalities can surface. Their purpose is to alert the individual to address his needs. However, too often the voices are interpreted as higher guides that should be obeyed, resulting in dangerous situations or real psychic disturbance.

The *animus* may be considered a sub-personality. *Animus* is a Jungian term for the woman's unconscious inner male. When repressed, this powerful, authoritarian figure rears its head and wants to be obeyed. When a woman has low self-esteem and has no sense of her own innate power, and at the same time is reaching up to the inner planes for direction while mired in emotional quicksand, she may contact the animus and mistake him for a 'spiritual guide'. The result is *animus obsession* or *possession*. In more severe cases where the woman is absolutely convinced she is being spiritually guided, psychiatric help may be called for. In other situations where the woman is open to understanding what is going on, counseling, which explains the reality and helps the subject toward raising self-esteem and empowering herself, will usually solve the problem.

Men, by the way, do not have this particular problem with their unconscious inner female, the *anima*, because she is not authoritarian. She presents other kinds of challenges to force a man to accept her as a partner.

Channeling

The word 'channeling' is commonly used today to imply communication from higher sources. Many people scoff at this, saying that it is impossible. Yet just as many believe that it is not only possible but completely reliable. The truth is probably somewhere between the attitude of the skeptic and that of the gullible. Strictly speaking, channeling is the ability to use one or more of the astral, mental, or intuitive senses. Its quality and reliability is totally dependent upon which senses are being used. Are they higher senses or the lower? Some writers call channeling only that which is from lower psychism, since 85-90% of all channeling is from this level. The effect of higher psychism is referred to by other phrases such as 'spiritual impression' or 'Soul impression'. This distinction is a good one, but not commonly made. So when 'channeling' is referred to, one must determine what actually is meant—and more precisely, what level of attunement is the psychic capable of making.

Alice Bailey describes the "types of guidance" available in *Esoteric Psychology II*. These range from the subconscious wish life of an individual to messages from spirits on the astral and mental planes to communication from a Master on the inner planes.

A relatively common occurrence in channeling, especially in the variety called mediumship, is that lesser developed psychics would usually not be aware when they are contacting a 'shade' or 'shell,' mistaking it for a living, conscious entity on an inner plane. A *shade* is a disintegrating astral body of someone who is dying to the astral and is moving on to the mental plane. The *shade* contains the former person's appearance, memory and idiosyncrasies which have been impressed in the astral body and are part of its dissipating substance. It is completely incapable of thought. The *shell* is but the further disintegration of the astral body, a stage beyond the shade. It is an astral corpse, but may be 'enlivened' temporarily by an elemental and may be made to appear like the person it was once part of, even possibly reproducing the person's characteristic handwriting.

Master D.K. says that no psychic power should be used until the Third Initiation is passed. The reason for this is that at this stage of development a person is sufficiently free from glamor and illusion so as to avoid harming another and deluding oneself.

We can only hope that those who use their psychic abilities prior to the Third Initiation are well motivated. It is usually not possible to convince a lower psychic to change his ways. Only by change in consciousness will the psychic choose to change his ways. As Master D.K. says,

> ...lower psychics are not easily reached and warned as they are ever determined that their clairvoyant and clairaudient powers are indicative of the advanced type of high spiritual unfoldment. Their minds are closed to all warnings and they function often behind a barrier of smug self-satisfaction. They forget that the aboriginal races and animals are all psychic and register that which the more mental types fail to record.[1]

To the inexperienced it is not always easy to tell the difference between channeling through lower psychism and channeling through higher psychism. Discrimination needs to be applied to determine the qualitative energy of the channeling. There are characteristics which might be helpful in assessing the nature of the channeling. Higher psychism involves the Soul in some way and therefore is loving, non-judgmental, meaningful, purposeful, inclusive, for the good of the whole, empowering, intelligent, creative and encouraging. The channel is always conscious during the channeling, acknowledges a higher power and is detached from both the material and the person if someone else is involved.

Lower psychism, on the other hand, may flatter, chastise, warn, threaten, demand obedience, and reflect greed, power or selfishness. It may conflict with personal ethics and universal spiritual principles. Pious platitudes and generalities are commonplace and the channel is frequently unconscious or semi-conscious.

Rending the Veils

There are protective non-physical barriers—called webs or veils—between the different bodies and dimensions and between the different subplanes. The veils are designed to protect the lower from being affected or consumed prematurely by the higher. The higher levels are of faster vibration and when the lower is not adapted to handle these more potent forces, their incursion can produce damage which may take even lifetimes to repair.

Expansion of consciousness must proceed gradually and naturally so that the vibration of the atoms of each level are changed to a higher rate—a higher quality. (Rate of vibration and quality are synonymous.) When the rate is sufficiently elevated the protective veil is penetrated and the next level is entered. Not understanding the care that must be

---

[1]Bailey, A.A., *Discipleship in the New Age*, Vol. I, 741.

exercised, many people wanting quick 'enlightenment' or more rapid progress using techniques which tear the veils, producing an inrush of higher energies. The immediate result appears to be beneficial, but the long-term consequences can be disastrous. Some common forcing techniques include drugs, intense breathing exercises, chanting and injudicious use of hatha and kundalini yoga. Veils can also be rent, both in individuals and in the bodies of humanity, through nuclear explosions, radioactivity, certain sounds and types of movement. During World War I the sounds of battle and the intense emotional strain of humanity tore the etheric web between the planetary etheric and astral planes. This intensified the emotional life on the physical plane, producing greater conflicts in many areas. This will speed up the change in consciousness, and usher in the age of brotherhood, sharing, love and understanding.

The webs and veils need to be penetrated, and we need to know how to do so safely. The guidelines are: pure motives, spiritual striving, idealism, meditation, alignment with the Self, and a life of sacrificial service.

The examples of what happens as a result of rending the veils are numerous. Torkom Saraydarian mentions some of these:

> ...when the web separating the etheric and astral planes is burned away by the increasing fire of the spiritual man, the three lower bodies, physical, emotional and mental, function as one unit. Greater unity is achieved when the web between the mental and Intuitional planes is burned away at the Fourth Initiation...
>
> The web between the second and third subplanes of matter prevents continuity of consciousness between the physical brain and the astral world. We are told that when a man reaches that point of development where he begins to see the fourth lower ether, the disintegration of this web starts and the man achieves continuity of consciousness between the physical brain and the astral world. He now has the right to work there to eliminate the sources of glamor and evil.
>
> Similarly, we have other webs on the second and third subplanes of the mental, Intuitional and Atmic planes. By eliminating these veils, continuity of consciousness is advanced from plane to plane, and finally man achieves continuity of consciousness with Monadic awareness. This is accomplished when the web between the second and third subplanes of the Atmic Plane is burned away. This is how the Antahkarana is built. Man at this point is awake on all planes of his microcosm through which he works and serves.[1]

---

[1]Saraydarian, T., *Psyche and Psychism*, 370. (Aquarian Educational Group).

X

THE ETHERIC BODY

Science is on the verge of a great discovery—that there are levels of life and consciousness in the physical realm which the senses cannot perceive. Esotericists have known this for thousands of years. Modern science needs to prove whatever it espouses as real, but now that infinitely smaller particles of matter are being discovered the etheric realms are being entered and the standards of proof are being challenged. Meanwhile, theories and hypotheses are being propounded where conventional proof is lacking. There will be no definitive statements about the existence of the etheric, but a gradual acceptance of the theories as valid statements about the subtle qualities of matter in the etheric-physical dimension. Physics is probably in the forefront of extending the boundaries of the physical into what was once considered to be 'meta'-physical. But we need not wait for widespread acceptance of what we know experientially to be fact.

How do we explain the fact that when a new pattern emerges in one place in a species through experiment, repetition or other influences, that pattern is found to emerge in another place without physical contact or similar influence? The skeptic says is does not happen. Experience tells us it does. We can give a facile explanation without further thought that it is simple telepathy. But what is that? Telepathy is communication from one consciousness to another. An easy explanation, but what does it imply?

For telepathy to exist, for one consciousness to communicate with another, there needs to be a medium or carrier of the communication. A physical medium such as air, for example, we know is incapable of carrying over distance learned behavior or attitudes. So there must be some more subtle medium which exists within and between objects or beings separated in space and yet capable of serving as a channel or network for transference of energy and communication content. Indeed such a medium does exist and we call it the etheric body or vital body.

The etheric exists in different grades of subtle energies and is considered to be part of the physical dimension or plane.

THE PHYSICAL PLANE

	Subplanes	Names	Plane Correspondences
Etheric	1	atomic	Monadic
	2	sub-atomic	Atmic
	3	super etheric	Buddhic
	4	etheric/ionic	Higher Mental
Dense Physical	5	gaseous	Lower Mental
	6	liquid	Astral
	7	solid	Physical

For convenience we usually refer to the Physical Plane in its two basic divisions: etheric (subplanes 1-4) and physical (subplanes 5-7).

Physical Plane Facts

1. The Physical Plane is unlike all the other planes in that it is not a principle. This means that nothing originates on this plane. It is a plane of effect only; it causes nothing—although there are immediate causes from one subplane to another. Therefore, in order to actually change anything on this plane, one must go to another plane. For example, if a person is physically ill, treatment must involve changing the cause at some other level. That cause is inevitably emotional and/or mental. Along with treatment at a causal level it is often advantageous to make some physical changes as well, particularly when a condition is chronic and 'fixed' in etheric-physical matter.

2. The etheric exists wherever the dense physical exists. Everything perceivable with our senses has an etheric counterpart—humans, plants, rocks, elements, air, planets, solar systems. So we can say that the etheric exists everywhere—in every space, place and time.

3. The etheric comprises the formative forces of the physical (dense physical). Whatever exists in the physical first exists in the etheric in time and space. For example, if you are going to have an accident tomorrow, your etheric body is already registering the effects of it because the inner cause is likely already present in your etheric. This is demonstrable through radionics. Or, if you are going to 'catch a cold' in two days, you already have the cold in your etheric body—again, because the causes are present.

There was a case where a patient was to be discharged from hospital, having recovered completely from some type of problem. A radionics practitioner, who had been working with the patient's doctor, advised the doctor against discharging his patient because the radionics analysis indicated that the patient was in a state of shock. The medical doctor, adept at assessing physical symptoms, rebuked the radionics practitioner for his error and dismissed the patient. Three days later the patient was back in hospital in a state of shock from an automobile accident.

Radionics is very sensitive on etheric levels. A device known as a radionics 'camera' is capable, as has been frequently demonstrated, of obtaining photographic images of the future growth of a seed, a fetus or any living, growing organism. It does this by penetrating to the etheric, causal level within the organism. Radionics work is most frequently done at a distance as well, attesting to the existence of an ubiquitous etheric network.

4. The time of transference from etheric cause to physical effect varies, depending upon such factors as:

- intensity of thought or emotion behind it,
- beneficial etheric influences present to mitigate negative effects,
- harmful etheric influences present to block positive effects,
- the nature of the transferring reality itself (e.g., influenza, cancer),
- the overall vitality of the etheric body,
- the general state of health of the dense physical body,
- the degree of integration that exists between the etheric and physical.

The degree of integration is determined by the attained level of consciousness of the individual. Prior to what is called the first Initiation there is but a tenuous consciousness-link between the etheric and dense physical, even though the life-link is obviously present. Transference of vitality related to consciousness is significantly lower, and only through long term or forceful presence of something on the etheric will the result be experienced in the physical. This may explain in part why some individuals can live in a very unhealthy way and still appear to remain physically quite healthy. If the behavior does not change, however, we often see the effects later in life.

After the first Initiation, which produces etheric-physical integration, transference from etheric cause to physical effect is much faster. We say such a person is more *sensitive*. With each subsequent Initiation, when first the astral body integrates with the etheric and then the mental body with the astral, the transference of emotion and thought to the physical body and external physical experiences takes place more and more rapidly—to the point where a thought can be physically experienced immediately. Fortunately our progression through the Initiations is determined by our purity. If it were not, and we gained such mental power to influence physical matter, we would destroy ourselves and our world.

5. The etheric is molded by:

—*Monadic essence*—the life force at the *atomic* level. Here are the *seed atoms*, including those from past lives, which give specific orientations for the development of the individual physical body.

—*Atmic substance*—the purpose, will and direction of the physical entity at the *sub-atomic* level.

—*Buddhic energy*—the archetypal blueprint for the individual, the life pattern or plan at the *super etheric* level. It can be strongly influenced by the astral body.

—*Higher Manasic matter*—the actual activity, more or less intelligent, which directs the denser atoms along one line or another. This is the *etheric* subplane per se, strongly influenced by thought and highly influential in determining physical well-being and behavior.

6. Etheric matter is extremely sensitive to thought. It is molded into forms by our thoughts. These become creative forces in the physical.

The creative Intelligence of the universe impresses Itself upon the etheric substance of this universe, causing the physical universe to operate and behave intelligently, lovingly and purposefully. It cannot do otherwise than the mind which controls it. The microcosm of our individual life follows the same principle. We cannot experience anything else but what we thoughtfully or thoughtlessly create within our own etheric bodies and within the etheric energies that surround us and our possessions. There is a consciousness-link (via the etheric) between other people and ourselves, between our 'things' and us. People approach us through our thoughts which fill the etheric space around us. They see us as we see ourselves since we color their perceptions of us. The things we own or possess also respond to the thoughts we impress on their etheric counterpart. The quality of these thoughts will either increase or decrease their vitality. This is especially true when the object is of an electro-magnetic nature because etheric energy is essentially electro-magnetic.

7. The etheric body has the same relationship to the physical as the Soul has to the personality.

8. The etheric body—planetary, human or otherwise—has three basic functions. It acts as:

—a receiver of energies,

—an assimilator of energies,

—a transmitter of energies.

The key to balance or good health in the body reflects this proper interchange of energies.

9. When a human being incarnates, the substance which is used to create the new etheric body is drawn from the etheric body of the earth, while the dense physical body is composed of the physical substance of the earth. This matter has been tainted by countless diseased bodies over millions of years and carries the seeds of three major diseases—syphilitic, tubercular and cancerous—which are called 'miasms' in homeopathic terminology. Miasms are etheric predispositions to the formation of a great variety of pathological conditions. They exist on the fourth etheric subplane in varying degrees of intensity and activity.

10. There are various factors which may inhibit the proper flow and assimilation of energies in and through the etheric body.

—*Miasms.* On the fourth etheric subplane miasms can be precipitated through bad falls, physical trauma or emotional shock producing pathological conditions.

—*Toxins.* These may be of a bacterial or chemical nature, residues from childhood diseases, drugs and pollutants of various kinds.

—*Physical anomalies* and diseased or traumatized areas.

—*Congestion.* This congestion may be objective—that is, miasmic or toxic—or it may be due to subjective factors of an emotional or mental nature found in the chakras or centers of force in the etheric bodies. Congestion may also be caused by electromagnetic imbalances, mineral deficiencies, and influences from such activities as the use of tobacco. Air pollution has a direct negative effect on the etheric body.

—*Over-stimulation.*

—*Lack of coordination* between the etheric body and the physical body such as we might find in conditions of epilepsy, debilitation, impotence, obsession and laryngitis.

Chakras, which are the energy pathways between the various bodies, can be damaged by traumas and shocks. Even constant fear, worry and anxiety can disturb the functional balance. Chakras are frequently blocked by our unbalanced living. When the blockage is at the entrance of the chakra, the energy is backed up to the astral or mental planes from which it originated, potentially causing psychological problems and/or endocrine dysfunction. When the blockage is at the point where the chakra exits to the physical body, a build up of energy can cause initial pressure followed by release into an endocrine gland producing erratic endocrine function with accompanying physical and psychological problems.[1]

---

[1] Cf. Tansley, D., *Radionics and the Subtle Anatomy of Man*, 21-28. (C.W. Daniel Co. Ltd.)

11. The etheric 'dimension' is a somewhat unorganized field of substance of four grades of matter vibrating between the gaseous state of physical matter and the lowest grade of astral substance. But when consciousness impresses it, it forms itself into a coherent body which is characterized by lines of force or minute strands of energy, not unlike the warp and woof of fabrics. Where these lines cross, important nodal points exist—significant energy exchange points. It is believed that homeopathic tissue salts have a beneficial effect on these points where they are not functioning efficiently. Where these lines cross each other twenty-one times we have major energy centers traditionally called *Chakras* (meaning whirling disks or wheels, but appearing more like vortices). There are seven such points in the human body. Other kingdoms of nature have fewer. Minerals have one chakra, plants two, and animals three. The average person has only five chakras operating, while the adept has seven.

There are twenty-one minor chakras where the energy strands cross fourteen times, and forty nine lesser points where the etheric lines of energy cross seven times. These and other tiny points may correspond to the acupuncture and acupressure points in the body.

The chakras have three main functions:

—*To vitalize the dense physical body.* The vitality is drawn from the general etheric dimension as well as from the etheric counterpart of air, water, food and other vitalizing substances. Vitality within the etheric body is also increased by rest and exposure to natural light. During sleep there is some separation of the etheric and dense physical bodies which revitalizes the etheric body.

—*To bring about the development of self-consciousness.* There is an important interplay among chakras in the etheric, emotional and mental bodies. The coordination of the chakras among these three bodies will definitely develop self-consciousness.

—*To transmit spiritual energy in order to bring the individual into a state of spiritual being.* For any energy or process to be complete it must go through three phases:
  - energy must be taken in;
  - it must be assimilated;
  - it must be expressed.

Spiritual progress does not occur by taking in and assimilating energy; a step towards spiritual being is marked only when the energy is transmitted or expressed. This is why service is the primary keynote of a Soul infused person. The chakras serve ideally on the physical plane for the manifestation and expression of received and assimilated energy in order to move one along the spiritual path.

THE SEVEN MAJOR CHAKRAS

Center	Sanskrit Name	Gland	Physical Area Governed
Crown/ Head	Sahasrara	Pineal	Upper brain, right eye, skin, skeletal structure, muscular system.
Brow	Ajna	Pituitary	Lower brain, eyes, (especially left eye), ears, nose, nervous system.
Throat	Vishuddha	Thyroid	Vocal apparatus, alimentary canal, respiratory system, shoulders, arms, neck, neck vertebrae, throat, mouth, teeth, gums, jaw.
Heart	Anahata	Thymus	Heart, blood, vagus nerve, circulatory system, respiratory system, shoulders, arms, ribs, breasts, upper vertebrae, immune system.
Solar Plexus	Manipura	Pancreas	Stomach, pancreas, liver, gall-bladder, abdomen, upper intestine, spleen, middle vertebrae, nervous system.
Sacral	Svadhisthana	Gonads	Reproductive system, lower intestine, lower vertebrae, pelvis, appendix, bladder.
Base	Muladhara	Adrenals	Kidneys, spinal column, legs, feet, hips, rectum, pelvis.

Base. This is the last center aroused in the development of consciousness. It is the center of planetary force in man, and the opposite pole to the crown center. It is the seat of Kundalini (coiled serpent) figuratively found in the base of the spine. It is the planetary energy of consciousness that slowly awakens in man. As it progresses up the spinal column, touching the root of each of the chakras, it awakens each of the centers in turn, until it finally connects with the crown center. This is the center of groundedness, physical safety and security, a sense of essential goodness and the basis of true power. The base is the home of the physical elemental.[1]

Sacral. It controls the sex life and must be transmuted to the throat center in the disciple. The energy of procreation becomes the pure energy of creation. A wise Teacher has indicated that this will remain a powerful

[1]See Chapter XII: Elementals.

center until two thirds of humanity is initiated. In consciousness terms it deals with control and power in relationships and physical concerns. It is therefore the center that governs business and finances. The big issues of power, control, money and sex are all centered here. The development of positive self esteem and an attitude of sharing are fundamental to growth at this level. The sacral is the home of the mental elemental.

Solar Plexus. This is the most active center in the average person at this time. It is the primary emotional center through which the emotional energy of the astral plane flows. It produces ambition and progress at first, and aspiration for enlightenment later. The energy here is basically one of reaction and must be lifted to the heart center where it becomes a compassionate and loving energy of response.

Cancer in the body is usually rooted in the dysfunction of this chakra. Issues relating to personal power are centered here. The so-called intuition that many people claim to have is in fact the functioning of survival intuition through the solar plexus where first impressions readily register and are found to be quite reliable. A sense of selfhood and self-confidence is produced as consciousness develops in a positive way at this level. This is the natural home of the astral elemental.

Heart. Its energy is magnetic and radiatory. It is brought into functioning activity after the Second Initiation. Its primary characteristics are that of compassion and love. For many healers and caregivers it is the principal center used. Developmentally it concerns the ability to give and receive love and attention. Allergies are ultimately heart-based problems.

Throat. This is the center of creative energy and creative intelligent expression as demonstrated by the present fifth Root-race. It is the place of the lower mind which is responsible for creating form. The development of personal expression is the consciousness of this chakra, especially the use of individual will power. Addictions are basically throat-centered issues.

Brow. When the personality is integrated and under the direction of the Soul, this center functions as the brow is the seat of the personality. After the third Initiation it is through this center that truth is directed. This is not truly the third eye although often referred to as such. The third eye is awakened after the third Initiation when the brow and head and alta major centers are awakened and functioning together as one unit, forming a triangle of light in the head. Through the brow we understand, we are able to perceive meaning and we see relationships between things. This is the place of the higher mind.

Head/Crown. This is the center of synthesis, the home of the Soul. With the consciousness of this center we know purpose, we perceive the 'group' and the universal truth. Its arousal brings perfection and the end of the cycle of rebirth. This occurs at the Fifth Initiation.

Chakra Structure

The Monadic extension and Soul reflection are found in the structure of every chakra. The Monad is the life of the atomic subplane, while the three aspects of the Soul—Will, Love and Intelligence—are the consciousness of the sub-atomic, super etheric and etheric, respectively. Each forms a level of the chakra or, since the chakras are usually portrayed as flowers (lotus in the East and rose in the West), each Soul quality is a tier of petals. The outer one—the Intelligence—is the first to unfold, the Love tier is the next, followed by the Will, and finally the life of the Monad is entered and movement to another dimension occurs.

Qualities		Etheric Levels
Life	(Monadic)	*atomic*—The central point of the vortex, gateway to other dimensions.
Will	(Soul)	*sub-atomic*—least active.
Love	(Soul)	*super etheric*—more active.
Intelligence	(Soul)	*etheric*—most active.

12. From an energy perspective all relationships can be perceived as positive-negative interactions. The positive is always the higher of the two; it is the cause of the negative activation and consequently is 'responsible' for it. This is why the human kingdom is positive to the animal kingdom and why we as humans are responsible for the animal kingdom. By virtue of the same principle, humanity is negative to the kingdom of Souls which is responsible for the human.

In terms of the bodies we can note the following typical energy polarities. (Positive is '+'; negative is '-').

	Male Person	Female Person
Atmic	+	-
Buddhic	-	+
Mental	+	-
Astral	-	+
Physical	+	-

Positive is *expressive* and negative is *receptive*. With integration of the bodies through development of consciousness, a synthesis occurs. Before integration, we note from the chart that the typical male is more expressive of will, mental characteristics and physical force, while the typical female is more expressive on intuitive and emotional levels.

The personality is determined by the gender of both the physical body and the mental body (which are always the same polarity). The male personality is positive (+), the female is negative (-). In terms of energy the male personality (+) relates to the Soul as female (-), and the female personality (-) relates to the Soul as male (+). The subconscious counterpart of the Soul in the male is also female (-)—'anima'—while the female subconscious polarity is male (+)—'animus'. We have, therefore, all the energy structures needed to bring about a balance and integration through dynamic energy relationships within each person and between people. Through the principle of projection, we relate to the opposite sex as 'our soul' and as 'our subconscious'. Therefore they can ideally help us in our evolutionary drive toward androgyny or synthesis.

The physical dimension also lends itself to similar analysis:

Subplanes	Energy
a. atomic	-
b. sub-atomic	+
c. super etheric	-
d. etheric	+
e. gaseous	-
f. liquid	+
g. solid	-

a. The *atomic* needs to be negative in order to receive impression from the Monad and other levels above itself, especially the mental.

b. The *sub-atomic* expresses the atomic in lower levels. Corresponding to the atmic plane of spiritual will, it gives the drive, direction and will to live.

c. The *super etheric* receives this energy and takes it deeply within itself as a unifying force and loving pattern. It is the power of coherence and unity and serves as a protector against the often disintegrating tendencies which creep into the fourth etheric level.

d. The *etheric's* purpose is to express the unity in intelligent forms on denser subplanes. Being positive, it can also be destructive. The opposing forces of integration-disintegration are often at war here and are automatically projected into denser matter.

e. The *gaseous* level receives openly the activity of the etheric state, giving it form.

f. The *liquid*, flowing as it is, is a perfect vehicle for expression into solid matter.

g. *Solid* physical matter is impressed with whatever influences impinge upon it.

Just as integration can and does occur between the various bodies of Man as consciousness expands and as a person masters the energy of each body, so a corresponding integration takes place in the subplanes of each body. For example, with emotional mastery comes control over the liquid subplane; with lower mental control comes meaningful direction of the gaseous state; with higher mental proficiency comes the wielding of higher power in the etheric subplane; and so on. (Study *The Physical Plane* chart at the beginning of this section on The Etheric Body.)

13. The etheric formative forces which give shape to dense physical matter are traditionally said to be composed of four basic elements: fire, air, water and earth. This fourfold composition has been translated into other terms by Dr. Guenther Wachsmuth who calls these formative forces: Warmth ether, Light ether, Chemical ether and Life ether. Each ether is said to produce different forms:

Ether	Forms	Subplane
Warmth	Spherical	Atomic
Light	Triangular	Sub-atomic
Chemical	Half Moon	Super etheric
Life	Square	Etheric

14. The etheric body is the vehicle of vitality for the physical entity. Vitality is also called *prana* in Sanskrit. This *prana* is said to exist as 'vitality globules' consisting of seven physical atoms each. These globules flash about in the atmosphere and can be seen by even those who are not particularly clairvoyant. Its usual appearance is that of a brilliant white or slightly golden light. Vitality of various grades and qualities enter into the body via the various chakras; from there they process through the spleen chakra where they are broken into streams of different colors as its atoms are whirled around the vortex of the spleen center, with each of its six spokes seizing one and the seventh color disappearing through the center of the vortex. The various rays, now separated, then go to different parts of the body to vitalize it.

Sleep is necessary to assimilate vitality or *prana*. This is most effectively done in the early part of the night when there is still plenty of vitality in the atmosphere which has been left behind by sunlight; by dawn it is almost completely exhausted. This may be one of the reasons why sick people frequently die at this time of night. This is also the basis for the old saying that one hour's sleep before midnight is worth two after.

When the splenic chakra cannot absorb *prana* from the atmosphere because of fatigue, illness or extreme old age, a person tends to absorb the etheric atoms from other people before they have extracted all the energy from the atoms. This is a natural kind of etheric vampirism. Plants also absorb this vitality, but seem to use only a small part, giving off the excess which man can then use.

Most people are not efficient users of vitality. Some teachers maintain that the use of meat, tobacco and alcohol inhibit the full utilization. While a pure physical life is obviously the best for the proper use of vitality, elevated thought and harmonious feelings help assimilate the vitality which is necessary for well-being.

15. The etheric chakras are intimately linked with their astral counterparts. When, through the stimulation of consciousness, they are more fully aroused, they bring into the physical body whatever quality the astral chakra contains. It becomes increasingly important for physical well-being to monitor the quality of one's emotional life.

16. The Sun in its trinitarian nature is a source of three kinds of energy, all of which we call 'fire' or electrical energy.

—The physical sun gives us vitality, *prana*.

—The Spiritual Sun gives us Life itself.

—The Heart of the Sun gives us the energy of consciousness. This is the energy of Universal Love.

When it meets matter there is a reaction or response. When matter reacts it creates, on its own level, an equal and opposite reaction. Hence the production of the positive and negative polarity of matter which we call *magnetism*. A magnetic field automatically produces a space between the opposites called a Bloch wall or a diamagnetic, non-spin energy state.

This diamagnetic space is where we do not experience the pull of the opposites, but can directly relate to states of consciousness or dimensions other than matter. Here, between the opposites, we can experience the universal love which, in a sense, is the absence of opposites or, in another sense, is the synthesis of opposites. Experiencing that love, we expand the diamagnetic space more and more, and increasingly neutralize the pull of the opposites or the pull of matter. Thus, we progressively respond to the electric fire of love from the heart of the sun. In this way we 'get out of ourselves' or more fully come into our Selves.

The anti-gravity of the non-spin state allows us to rise up to higher levels and ascend the 'Mount of Vision' to perceive what the Soul is and knows and sees.

Nature has provided us with the diamagnetic centers in our bodies. These are called chakras. These centers provide us with the opportunity to move into other states of consciousness where we can experience different aspects of love that are indicated by the nature of each chakra. They are but different pathways to contact the One.

In another vein, these diamagnetic centers are also located in various places in the earth body. They are noted for the phenomena produced in them, such as the disappearances of people, planes and objects that occur there. They are also characterized by a relative lack of gravity, enabling individuals or things to be levitated easily. Such a center may have existed where the great pyramids were constructed enabling these pyramids, composed of enormously heavy stone, to be constructed with ease.[1]

Basic Requirements for a Healthy Etheric-Physical Body

1. Adequate exercise.
2. Sufficient rest—relaxation periodically through the day and sleep at night.
3. Nutritious diet.
4. Proper breathing.
5. Cleanliness—internal and external.
6. Light—preferably natural sunlight.

These six guidelines, combined with positive thought and uplifting emotions assure one of a healthy body. The foundation of enlightenment is in the physical body. We need to take good care of it and use it both as a springboard to higher states and as a vehicle through which the higher can be purely expressed. To be well is also our duty to the rest of humanity.

Etheric Influences

Our own etheric bodies are not isolated from the etheric body of humanity, the earth, and everything else around us. We are constantly affected by our environment, just as whatever we do and are affects our environment.

---

[1]Cf. Childress, D. H., *Anti-gravity And The World Grid*. (Adventures Unlimited Press/Publisher's Network).

Many influences have a direct or indirect impact on etheric bodies. Some have a beneficial effect, while others have a deleterious effect. Some influences occur naturally, while others are man-made.

Sunlight. As previously mentioned, sunlight is probably the most energizing and vitalizing influence on all etheric bodies in the solar system. Excess on the human body causes over-stimulation and deterioration, so moderation should prevail. Through gradual adaptation increased exposure can be tolerated beneficially.

Fluorescent lighting. Most fluorescent lighting, which is not full spectrum, produces an unhealthy response in the etheric body because it emphasizes certain unnatural frequencies and excludes the balance of a full spectrum such as is obtainable from natural lighting or sunlight.

Sound. Both sound and color, as well as light, generally have a direct effect on the third and fourth etheric subplanes and so can be either harmful or beneficial. Of particular benefit are the sounds of nature such as wind, flowing water, birds chirping, etc. Uplifting and harmonious music also has a revitalizing effect, whereas noise, discordant music, and music such as heavy rock have a negative and disorganizing effect on the etheric bodies, whether these be of humans or other kingdoms of nature.

Many experiments have been done to show the beneficial effect of playing certain types of classical music for plants. Plants have been found to respond very well to such music, growing faster and stronger because of its influence.

Color. Color therapy can be used very beneficially to affect positive changes in the etheric body, and therefore is used increasingly for promoting physical well being. Sunglasses or tinted glasses often cause weakness in a person's etheric body because light is being channeled through one specific color which may not be required or beneficial for the individual and, in fact, may increase a particular vibration that is already strong or too strong.

Water. Pure water contains a great amount of *prana* or vitality and is an excellent source of energy for etheric bodies. Bathing in water, especially salt water, which seems to stabilize the positive-negative balance within the etheric body, is very helpful. Showering is also very beneficial, possibly due to the increased negative ions that are generated from falling water. We know that positive ions, when in excess, have a negative effect on the etheric body; likewise negative ions appear to regenerate it. Drinking pure water, especially solarized water, brings added vitality to the etheric body. Water can be solarized simply by putting it in a clear glass container and leaving it in sunlight for a matter of minutes or hours.

In this way not only is the *prana* increased but there is also a full spectrum color influence which can help to balance any depletion of specific color in the etheric body.

Magnetic energy fields. There are many fluctuations in the earth's etheric body due to extra-planetary and intra-planetary causes. These result in all kinds of reactions in humans as well as in animals, ranging from ill health to relationship problems to psychological fluctuations. Earthquakes and atmospheric changes produce alterations in the etheric body. Rawls and Davis[1] have extensively studied the effects of magnetism on bodies and have developed certain procedures which can be used therapeutically to restore magnetic imbalances within the etheric body.

But there are many applications of magnetic energy which can be disturbing. We know, for example, that the north pole of a magnet placed at the right ear causes weakness, just as putting the south pole of a magnet at the left ear does. Because of magnetics in telephone receivers, people who use the telephone for many hours of the day can cause an imbalance by always holding the receiver to the same ear.

Noxious rays. There are many sources of disturbing rays such as underground streams, x-rays, radar, CB radios, high tension electrical lines, electrical generators and Extremely Low Frequency (E.L.F.) waves. These waves of specific frequencies are increasingly found in many electrical devices and are even deliberately produced, potentially creating extreme disturbance in the etheric body and therefore potentially in the entire individual.

Air. Pure air is an increasingly rare commodity on this planet because of increased air pollution and the depletion of forests and vegetation. Fresh air is highly energizing, while pollutants can leave toxic residues in the etheric body producing reactions, often allergic, and physical illness.

Clothing. Some people are disturbed by synthetic substances worn next to the skin. Their vibration is alien to the natural vibration of the body. It is advisable to wear clothing made of natural substances close to the skin.

Vitamins and minerals. These minute building blocks of the physical body are in fact important sources of nutrients for the etheric body. Synthetically produced vitamins and minerals are significantly less energizing to the etheric body. These nutrients should be taken in their natural state, such as in raw foods, or, if taken as supplements should be made from natural substances and prepared with a minimal amount of disturbance

---

[1]Cf. *The Magnetic Blueprint of Life, The Magnetic Effect, Magnetism And Its Effects On The Living System, The Rainbow In Your Hands* .

from heat, mixing, etc. Less sensitive people, who have less integration between the etheric and dense physical body, can benefit equally from synthetic vitamins and minerals which then have a more direct effect on the dense physical body and less on the etheric levels.

Posture. Certain yoga postures and movements enhance the energy flow in various parts of the body; this is also true of such movements as Tai Chi and dance. Carrying and holding the physical body in a natural and balanced posture allows vitality to flow through the etheric body and into the physical much more freely. Smiles increase the positive flow, while frowns decrease it. Healthy exercise is also very beneficial. Even when feeling tired a modicum of exercise can restore a feeling of high energy. This would be true when the tiredness has not been caused by over-stimulation such as overwork but by congestion due to a lack of expression of energy.

Stress. When there are external influences or internal influences from the mind or emotions which overload the etheric body's ability to express what it has been impressed by, there is a blockage or congestion which occurs in the etheric body. The flow of beneficial creative energies are thereby impeded.

Social environment. The people around us can stimulate us to excess, creating stress. They can also drain our vitality by taking from us more than what we are really capable of giving without depleting ourselves. At times we need to remove ourselves from such influences, and when that is not possible we need to use our will to protect ourselves from depletion.

Physical environment. Order in our immediate environment is very important for etheric harmony. Our etheric energies can be much more harmonious when we live in an ordered space and work in a tidy space. The presence of plants in our work and living spaces can also be very beneficial. Ferns, for example, can have a very peaceful, calming influence on our etheric bodies. We need to have sufficient spaces in our life where there is a lack of noise, confusion and activity so that our vitality can be restored as needed.

Tobacco. Smoking tobacco has a direct effect on the etheric body. Smoking usually creates a congestion in the etheric body, blocking a freer expression of etheric energies into the dense physical. If an individual has a loose connection between the etheric and dense physical a little smoking can cause a closer connection. However, since most people because of stress, are already experiencing a very tight connection between the etheric and physical bodies, smoking tobacco simply aggravates the condition and causes more stress.

Flower essences. Bach and California flower essences are commonly used to treat conditions in various bodies. Some have a direct influence on the etheric body. For example, if a person has experienced shock of any kind the use of Rescue Remedy can prove very helpful.

Teslar devices. These devices, sometimes found in wrist watches, are specifically designed to restore a natural frequency to the etheric body. The natural frequency of the earth and the human body is close to 7.8 hertz; the teslar devices produce a similar frequency and thus maintain a small energy field that is healthy and natural around the body, blocking vibrations that may be sufficiently different that they could weaken the natural energy field.

Gems. Each precious or semi-precious stone has a specific vibration and produces a particular effect on the etheric body. Gem therapy is often used to restore specific weaknesses or imbalances within the etheric body. Crystals are now increasingly being used as a means of vitalizing as well as expressing energies, and can also be used for healing purposes.

Laying on of hands. There are various forms of healing currently being used, such as polarity therapy, massage, rolfing, etc. which all have specific effects on the etheric and dense physical bodies. Whenever laying on of hands is used, whatever its form, it is the etheric body through which the physical body is being affected.

Blessing. By blessing our food, our work, or anything, we impose a positive thought form on that which we bless, and at the same time we invoke positive elementals and positive higher beings, thus creating a potentized energy field for the benefit of all.

It is impossible to avoid all the external influences that disturb or weaken our etheric bodies. Therefore, we are reminded that the answer to total harmony, well-being, and balance lies within ourselves. Being centered in a loving attitude to all, protects us and generates greater positive vibration than any interfering influences around us. To be in loving relationship is always the purpose of our quest and growth in consciousness. There is no reason to fear outside influences. Etheric energies are controlled by thought and therefore our own etheric bodies respond to the thoughts we think and the feelings we have. Let us attempt to make those thoughts positive, strong and loving, producing a healthy body. 'As you think in your heart, so are you.' Mental control over our bodies requires discipline. Basically, discipline is following the rhythms, energies and radiations of the Soul. As we do this in our practical daily living the etheric body becomes more and more magnetic, thus more sensitive to spiritual ideas, energies and realities.

For survival, the etheric body of every living organism responds to the strongest influence in its environment. Let us create the external environment as well as the internal environment which we want to experience physically. Let us create highly beneficial influences with the powers that we have. Since so much of our expression and interaction with others is through speech let us use our voices in therapeutic ways. The voice can either raise or lower the life energy or vitality of others. Our voices are therapeutic and energizing when our brain hemispheres are balanced, when our own vitality is high when we are speaking, and when our intent, out of love or concern, is to strengthen.

Conclusion

From the far reaches of space to the smallest atomic particle there is total interconnectedness. Nothing in the created and creative universe is outside of the etheric matrix which holds everything in a state of relatedness. There is constant communication between all the parts of the universe through the energy network which vivifies every aspect of this awesome body of life and consciousness. There is only ONE LIFE, pouring through the variety of forms through which it expresses itself; the only differences are those in consciousness. As our consciousness expands we abandon the illusion of separateness and enter more fully and more responsibly into living the Will, the Love, and the Intelligent Activity of the One Life in Whom we live and move and have our being.

XI

THE PSYCHIC SENSES

Every body, or coherent energy field, exists in relation to other bodies within the one body of humanity and within the one body of planetary life. In order for a body to be in relationship it must have the vehicles or means through which energy connections can be made and maintained. These vehicles for energy exchange are the *senses* found in each body. The senses enable us to receive as well as express energy.

We are familiar with the five physical senses, but are we equally aware that there are equivalent senses in our astral, mental and intuitive bodies? And if we do not know that they exist, is it likely that we will use and develop them? Hardly. If we do not use them it becomes virtually impossible to express ourselves adequately on astral, mental and intuitive levels. The aspiration to wholeness and the urge to self-improvement must be accompanied by awareness and conscious development of ourselves at different levels. Knowing about all of our senses gives us many more opportunities to unfold our potentials as whole and complete beings, and provides us with the means of cultivating closer and more meaningful relationships with other beings with whom we are united in the One Life we share.

Our senses are vehicles of consciousness, enabling us to perceive and interact with the parts and the whole, with inner aspects of ourselves and the inner aspects of the One Self.

Physical Senses

The physical senses—sight, hearing, smell, taste and touch—are usually perceived as receptors rather than transmitters, but closer examination will show that they are also vehicles whereby we express ourselves in the physical world. They are the means through which our True Self is grounded in the outer world, so the personal use of these senses must be guided by the principles governing the nature of the Self. They must be used responsibly to produce harmony, creativity, nourishment, etc.—in short, in intelligent activity.

The five senses are not unique to the human kingdom—they are the senses of our animal body. The human body actually has seven senses, two of these being peculiar to human nature. They can be called 'common sense' and 'direct perception' and are a result of the human Soul (which is distinct from the animal soul) and its influence on the human brain.

The sixth sense, *Common Sense*, develops in more advanced human beings when the lower mind is sufficiently coordinated with the brain, enabling it to form relatively enlightened conclusions from integrating all the relevant sensory input. It is a sense of meaningful relationships.

The seventh sense, *Direct Perception*, develops when the higher mind coordinates with the brain through the lower mind, producing a synthetic view of life and its purpose in form, based upon sensory information and etheric sensitivity (which provides an awareness of immediate causes). Soul intent and purpose is communicated via the brain.

Each sense corresponds to a specific subplane of the etheric-physical body. It will be noted that the senses actually exist in etheric matter, even though the sense *organs* are all found in solid physical matter.

Subplane	Physical Sense
(Soul—Brain)	Direct Perception
(Soul—Brain)	Common Sense
Atomic	Smell
Sub-atomic	Taste
Super etheric	Sight
Etheric	Touch
Gaseous	Hearing

When a person undergoes a general anesthetic, the etheric body separates from the dense physical body. The two, however, are still linked by the life-thread which does not become severed until death. Many people who undergo surgery under a general anesthetic report that the consciousness continues, but outside the physical body. They could often hear what was being said by the people present and they could see what was going on. Similar reports are given by people in deep hypnotic trance.

Non-Physical Senses

The following chart lists seven senses for each of the planes/bodies. The highest two astral and Intuitive senses are not traditional teaching, but are this author's suggestion for completing the tabulation. The words suggest a kind of energy which exists at those levels. The physical senses are listed to show their correspondences in the other bodies, and to hint as to the possible meaning of the non-physical senses.

Physical	Astral	Mental	Intuitional
Direct Perception	(At-one-ment)	Spiritual Telepathy	(Bliss)
Common Sense	(Higher Devotion)	Response to Group Vibration	(Adoration)
Smell	Emotional Idealism	Spiritual Discernment	Idealism
Taste	Imagination	Discrimination	Intuition
Sight	Clairvoyance	Higher Clairvoyance	Divine Vision
Touch	Clairsentience	Higher Clairsentience	Healing
Hearing	Clairaudience	Higher Clairaudience	Comprehension

Astral Senses

The lowest three astral senses are equally shared with the animal kingdom. *Imagination*, however, is peculiarly human. It is the result of the lower mind's ability to create thought-forms which are energized when they are impressed on the astral body. Imagination can be positive and creative or negative and destructive. It is positive when the lower mind creates an accurate thought-form, faithful to the ideal at a higher mind level, and the astral body clothes it in its energy without reaction. In other words, there is emotional *response* rather than emotional *reaction*. Imagination is negative when it is impressed with a distorted thought or when there is emotional reaction. A negative product of the imagination could be a fantasy, worry, exaggeration or any type of unreality/illusion.

Emotional Idealism, and what we might call *Higher Devotion* and *At-One-Ment*, are a direct result of Soul Consciousness operating on the higher subplanes of the astral body.

Clairaudience. This is the ability to hear astral sound waves—the feeling tone of physical sounds (words, noise, music). It literally means 'clear hearing', and can refer to hearing the voices of the emotional 'sub-personalities' we all have as part of our subconscious. The communication from astral entities ('spirits') can also be heard.

There are sounds everywhere, but we are not usually aware of them because our ears have a limited range of perception (15-20,000 vibrations per second). When we use clairaudience, after we have developed higher senses, we can consciously tune in to a wide range of sounds emanating from such sources as flowers blooming, gemstones radiating or leaves changing color. Wherever there is energy moving or change taking place, there is sound. The development of higher senses and Soul consciousness gives us the power to direct our clairaudience (or clairvoyance and clairsentience) at will. This control is necessary to avoid astral sensory overload and emotional breakdown.

Clairsentience. This word literally means 'clear feeling'—feeling as in 'touch'—and is often called 'psychometry' when referring to 'reading' the impressions from objects. All etheric and astral bodies contain the records of past experience and present feelings. These impressions can be touched by another's emotional body and felt. If there is a sufficient astral-mental connection in the experience, the feeling can be described in words, giving some kind of meaning to the experience. Without discrimination and spiritual discernment, this sense alone cannot reveal purpose, meaning, motivation, intention and the like, so it is extremely limited. It does, however, enable us to go outside of ourselves and feel our environment and know what others feel, thus extending the limits of our relationships.

Clairvoyance. Meaning 'clear seeing', clairvoyance enables us to see astral forms. Our eyes normally register waves of 800—390 millicrons in length, restricting vision to a rather limited field. When clairvoyance is used we can see both etheric and astral forms. (One should not be misled by the occasional etheric sight caught out of the corners of one's eyes. Here there are cells called rods which are sensitive to faint light and therefore to the fourth etheric subplane.) With clairvoyance we can see the forms of desires, feelings, fears, emotional reactions, and the various entities found on the astral plane. We are also sensitive to the images created by imagination and the formless colors of the astral plane. When some people begin to develop this sense they often report seeing colors, but have no idea what they mean or represent.

These lower three senses are very common because they are part of our animal nature. We depend on them so much in our daily relationships that we take them for granted, using them quite unconsciously. People who use them more consciously are often called *psychic*. These three senses should not be relied upon for accuracy. They are highly subjective and always tainted with personal bias, limitation and selfishness. They should not be used to guide others until the mental senses have been developed.

Imagination. Imagination is our 'image-making' sense on the astral plane, enabling the mind to cast its influence in astral matter. Imagination 'tastes' the quality of feeling in things. Unfortunately it is more often used for lower things rather than higher realities emanating from Intuitive or Higher Mind levels. 'Creative imagination' is the highest form of this sense. We possess it when the Thinker (the Soul) can impress it with the truth, beauty and goodness of Itself. When we use creative imagination we create appropriate images of the evolutionary Plan and the Divine Purpose.

Emotional Idealism. When we are emotionally oriented toward some higher ideal we are transmuting desire into aspiration. When the higher reality on the mental or Intuitive plane is contacted, the atoms of the astral body become oriented toward it, making the astral body very receptive and impressionable. This is called aspiration. This is the *first sense* of the higher astral and is therefore more expressive and dynamic. (The previous sense, imagination, is transitional between higher and lower, and has the dual nature of expression and impression. The lowest three senses are more receptive than expressive. These differences between the levels are characteristic of all higher and lower levels of any category, body or being anywhere—the lower are always more receptive and 'taking', while the higher are always more expressive and 'giving'. This is a universal principle.)

Emotional idealism, controlled and directed by the Higher Mind, gives one a fiery enthusiasm to act intelligently for the benefit of others in some type of service, and it leads to the next posited sense, 'devotion'.

Devotion. When the astral body is polarized toward the Intuitive Plane, which it naturally seeks when the Ideal is experienced, it comes in contact with Divine Love as the Idea or the Plan. Devotion, dedication and worship result from Love's presence. Devotion is a total emotional giving to the Idea, the god, the cause or creative deity of one's being.

At-one-ment. With devotion there is still separation. There is the lover and the Beloved. With at-one-ment there is emotional/astral union, there is identification with the life of the Beloved. Through sacrifice the personal desires (personal will) have been transfigured by the union with Divine Will. Universal Purpose is known and lived through the astral body.

There is a correspondence between the astral senses and the planes of existence. If you recall the principal characteristics of the planes you will see how the astral senses serve the totality of one's being.

ASTRAL SENSES

Sense	Plane	Quality of the Plane
(At-one-ment)	Atmic	Will, Purpose, Unity
(Devotion)	Buddhic	Love, Meaning, Plan
Emotional Idealism	Higher Mental	Plane of ideals, Intelligent Activity
Imagination	Lower Mental	Form creation
Clairvoyance	Astral	Plane of mirrored images, colorful forms
Clairsentience	Etheric	Seat of the senses
Clairaudience	Physical	Sound

Mental Senses

The lowest four mental senses are part of the lower mind, the higher three forming the senses of the higher mind. For want of better terms, the lower three senses are called by the same name as the corresponding senses of the astral body, but qualified by 'higher'.

Higher Clairaudience. This sense enables us to register thoughts associated with the mental, astral or physical planes. We can 'hear' the sound waves of the four lowest mental subplanes within ourselves and others. We are therefore sensitive to both conscious thoughts and unconscious thought-forms. This is simple mental telepathy—mind to mind communication. When more developed, it enables us to communicate telepathically with the Soul.

Higher Clairsentience. Feeling the quality of thought through higher clairsentience enables us to touch the soul in any form, as *quality* and *soul* are synonymous. This sense is sometimes called 'Planetary Psychometry' because it enables us to come in contact with the mind of the Planet—to be aware of its past and present conditions as well as its future possibilities. This includes ideas created by collective meditations, shared visions and progressive thought.

Higher Clairvoyance. This mental form of clairvoyance enables us to see thought-forms, both in their shape and outer effects and in their structure and inner dynamics. Operating through the brow (Ajna) center, higher clairvoyance connects the optic nerves, etheric brain and mental centers. Contact can be made with sources of information from what is referred to as higher plane libraries and books. When highly developed, this sense heightens reasoning ability and provides for a closer contact with one's Inner Guide. The formative forces from the fourth mental subplane can be perceived as geometric forms and symbols, revealing some of the causes of physical and astral events.

Discrimination. Influenced by the comparable sense in the Intuitional Body—Intuition itself—discrimination is the ability to differentiate between reality and non-reality, Self and not-Self, truth and illusion, cause and effect, and the various sources of impression. With discrimination we can finally determine what is essentially right and wrong. Prior to developing this sense our judgments of right and wrong are determined by past conditioning and selfish motive. Now we can see what furthers spiritual evolution and what blocks it. That which is a support is right; that which hinders is wrong.

Spiritual Discernment. The essential sense for learning the Science of Impression, spiritual discernment is a Soul sense. It is a faculty for knowing the causes, Ideas and Archetypes that emanate from the 'heart of God', the group Soul. The sources and levels of all impressions registering on the mental or astral planes can be accurately discerned. The truth can be known.

Response to Group Vibration. Soul-infused groups and groups on higher planes (such as Hierarchy) emit vibrations. These vibrations are the radiations from the Soul of the group, and indicate the particular ray quality and characteristics of the group. This sense enables an individual to respond to these group vibrations and be affected by them. One may:

—be energized for service on the inner planes,
—be supported for active service on the outer planes,
—have increased energy to meet one's own true needs,
—be stimulated to greater creativity,
—be purified from any lingering illusions,
—be aligned with the group's plans, intentions and activities.

Spiritual Telepathy. Response to group vibration is a very high level contact with Soul, but there is still a hint of separation between the Source of vibration and the one who registers or responds to that vibration. With spiritual telepathy the union between Soul and Soul is more complete; figuratively speaking we say that Soul communicates with Soul. The basis of communication is so equal and so transcendent of time and space, that there is virtually no separation. The union between Souls is sufficiently complete to be able to serve the planetary Life and Will along with members of the planetary Hierarchy.

The correspondence between the mental senses and the planes of existence can be seen in the following tabulation.

MENTAL SENSES

Sense	Plane	Quality of the Plane
Spiritual Telepathy	Atmic	Will, Life, Purpose, Unity
Response to Group Vibration	Buddhic	Love, Meaning, Plan, Intention, Heart
Spiritual Discernment	Higher Mental	Truth, ideals, source
Discrimination	Lower Mental	Differentiation, parts
Higher Clairvoyance	Astral	Mirrored images and forms
Higher Clairsentience	Etheric	Mental impressions, quality forces
Higher Clairaudience	Physical	"In the beginning was the Word"— sound

Intuitional Senses

As we enter the realms of the Buddhic Plane with its Intuitional senses words begin to fail; they but point to experiences of unity. As the old Zen saying goes, 'pointing the finger at the moon, is not the moon'. The senses of this body are beyond mind; they can be seen as faculties of the Heart and the means whereby the Spirit or Monad can express Itself as Love in the worlds below Itself.

Comprehension. With comprehension we go beyond linear reason; we understand without drawing conclusions from a series of observations; we know without accumulating facts. Comprehension is direct knowledge; it is a synthetic way of knowing all-at-once, simultaneously from all viewpoints. We know the effects, their causes, and the laws and principles operating. This is the 'knowing Heart' attuned to the planetary Soul.

Healing. In ordinary daily practice healing involves a removal of disturbing symptoms, the reduction of pain, or the elimination of disease. The effects of this practice are always temporary. Disease, illness, and pain are symptoms of misalignment with the Soul, so any true healing must restore the harmonious relationship between personality and Soul.

When healing from the Intuitional Plane we create harmony between the different levels of one's being and establish rhythm (the highest state of energy). Healing in this highest sense cannot be done without first developing all the mental senses. The highest mental sense, *Spiritual Telepathy*, enables one to serve and communicate the Planetary Life. Healing depends upon this ability because it restores the individual or group to its rightful place within the Planetary Life. We, as individuals, do not exist for ourselves. The whole reason for our being in incarnation is to fulfill our function for the evolution of the Planetary Being. Intuitional healing does not require any specific form or technique. Healing occurs through the loving radiation of the healer who may be either present or absent. The healer's response is determined by a wide range of factors within the individual to be healed. The healer will always know the right time so as not to interfere in any necessary work the subject must do. The goal of healing on a personal level is to put one in touch with one's own true Self. Whatever the healer needs to do to achieve that objective is possible from the Intuitional Plane.

Divine Vision. Vision on the Intuitional plane is called 'Divine' because it is only possible after the Third Initiation when a person has achieved union with the Soul. This is a transcendence of purely human nature and an entering into Divine nature. At this time three head centers interact, creating a triangle of light, producing 'enlightenment' or 'illumination'. This triangle is the true 'third eye' which gradually moves from the center of the head and seats itself in etheric matter at the brow center. Divine Vision is the use of this third eye, which enables one to be aware of profound inner realities and mysteries and communicate them to humanity in ways that uplift, heal and transform.

Third eye capabilities include the power to create and direct energy in a masterful way, producing results according to intention and aligned with divine purpose and plan. Divine vision is a result of true aspiration and manifests when a person is truly capable of selfless service for humanity.

Freed from illusion and purified in motives, the Initiate who possesses Divine Vision sees Reality clearly.

Intuition. Intuition is that faculty by which "Self recognizes its own essence in and under all forms."[1] Intuition does not mean the same as its customary usage of 'gut feeling' or 'hunches', or even astral sensing with which it is often confused. It is the sense of seeing and knowing the whole of everything in which there is no separation. To the mortal mind this is perfect wisdom and to the mortal heart this is perfect love. Intuition synthesizes everything to its essence and reveals the essence as the Self.

Idealism. From the perspective of the personality the level on which this sense operates is the source of all thought, the archetypal level of Ideas, Divine Ideas. From the Intuitional Plane perspective it is that too, but not as an originating source. Idealism is the sense which receives impressions from even higher levels—essentially from Divine Will—and translates them into ideas which form the Divine Plan—the Plan of the Planetary Hierarchy. Through idealism the Divine Purpose is known and

---

[1]Bailey, A.A., *A Treatise on Cosmic Fire*, 201.

one enters the Mind of God—the Planetary Being. Through idealism, Purpose and Plan are precipitated into the mind of Man for intelligent and wise action.

Adoration. This sense develops in the union one has with the Heart of the Planetary Being, resonating with the Heart of the Sun. 'The Son of God' is the embodiment of the love of God, and the result of this great, all consuming love. The advanced Initiate stands in adoration of the One Life, and radiates this Life as Love to all other beings.

Bliss. This is the sense of glorious union with the One Life. The Initiate is a virtual source of life for all before moving on to higher work and greater responsibility. He is beyond the need to incarnate, having reached the Fifth or Sixth Initiation.

As with the astral and mental senses, so too with the Intuitional senses there are revealing correspondences with the planes of existence:

INTUITIONAL SENSES

Sense	Plane	Quality of the Plane
Bliss	Atmic	Life
Adoration	Buddhic	Love, Ideals
Idealism	Higher Mental	Light, Ideals
Intuition	Lower Mental	Self in forms
Divine Vision	Astral	Reflection of love
Healing	Etheric	Formative forces aligned
Comprehension	Physical	All things NOW

Conclusion

In our look at the senses we have simply mapped the journey we are on. While we may aspire to higher levels since we know what rewards await us there, we need to remind ourselves to be fully present at the level on which we are now functioning. We need to use the senses we have developed or are developing in better and more responsible ways. Our senses are for service, so if we use them appropriately the higher senses will naturally unfold.

Each of us is focused on a particular level of our being, and processes information through that level naturally and automatically. For one it might be through the astral, for another the lower mental, and for others the higher mental or the Heart.

Whatever the level, there is no indication of being more advanced or less advanced than another person focused on a different level.

To be focused on a particular level does not mean that a person is fully conscious at that level. It simply means that the Soul has need of experiencing life dominantly through that level at the sacrifice of some other level—until it chooses a period of life in which it will function through the various other levels in a more integrated way.

Knowledge can be gained through any level but wisdom is attained only through experience at the appropriate level. For example, you can have knowledge of the Chakras, but you can have no wisdom about them unless you consciously experience their activity and know what you are experiencing.

Experience without knowledge does not lead to wisdom any more than does knowledge without experience. Experience is concrete; knowledge is abstract. Wisdom combines the two into a whole. Wisdom is the incarnation of Ideas.

So regardless of where you are primarily focused, you always need to go to other levels for either knowledge or experience.

The only exception to all this is when a person is an integrated personality aligned with the Soul. This stage can be seen as a person completes the Third Initiation when illusion has been overcome.

Everything in our experience has many levels of meaning and many levels to which we can relate. So it is impossible to have an exhaustive or perfect knowledge of anything.

The ultimate grasp of any reality comes through union with it—that is the process of *experiencing*. The union, when complete, is an absolute merging where the observer and the observed, or the experiencer and the experience, cannot be differentiated. They are one and the same.

XII

ELEMENTALS

Few people know they have elementals and fewer still know how to relate to them. We all have a physical elemental, an emotional elemental and a mental elemental because we have physical, emotional and mental bodies. The elementals may be viewed as the embodied natural life force or intelligence of each body. They are the aggregate of the tiny atomic and cellular lives of the bodies. These elementals are involutionary rather than evolutionary, but nevertheless have a unique basic intelligence. Elementals have no form of themselves, assuming the form of the conditions in which they exist. The sum of the elementals within a person comprise the 'lower personality' and in a sense stand in opposition to the Soul and all it represents, providing the necessary tension for growth.

Elementals know how to maintain healthy bodies and work to do so despite the ego's interference. Although we believe these bodies to be ours, they are equally the bodies of elementals who often care for them better than we do.

Torkom Saraydarian describes the nature of the more developed types:

> The elementals have a certain degree of intelligence, and when they are advanced they do not like it when you are doing wrong to them. An advanced physical elemental wants you to eat vegetables and fruits, keep clean, and have enough rest and fun. An advanced astral elemental does not like gossip and cheap excitements; it does not like the vibration of hatred and fear, but likes joy, love and philanthropic feelings. If the mental elemental is advanced it likes hard work, serenity, beauty, and the vibration of higher ideas and visions.
>
> If you do things that the elemental does not like, it expresses its dislike by causing you trouble in the form of sickness, depression and confusion.[1]

Elementals, not having self-consciousness, actually cannot like or dislike. Saraydarian is really saying that when we do things contrary to the basic

---

[1]Saraydarian, T., *Psyche & Psychism*, 118-119. (Aquarian Educational Group.)

natural well-being of any of our bodies there is a negative reaction within the affected body.

Because the elementals are the natural intelligence of our bodies, one should consider them when attempting any kind of healing. The elemental of each body can be imaged in any manner (e.g., a cartoon character, an animal, a wise old woman, etc.) and directly addressed. You may ask the elemental what the problem is and what action would ameliorate the situation. Like the devas, elementals are affected by sound, color, light, movement and especially love. Using these means wisely, a great rapport can be established, resulting in improved health and well-being.

The quality of elementals which constitute our bodies is determined by the degree of advancement or consciousness we bring to our incarnation. We may have lower or higher elementals as a result of our status. In any and all cases it is our responsibility to help develop and evolve these pre-conscious beings on their path toward becoming human monads.

With lesser developed elementals in our respective bodies we have varying degrees of the following conditions.

Physical—inertia; laziness; sense gratification; response to appetite; desire for physical pleasure and comfort. The required response on the part of the intelligent and caring person is to learn to sacrifice and respond to the *goodness* in life through *giving*.

Astral—stimulation of the emotions without regard for quality; strong reactions; intense desires; mood swings. The appropriate training in this case involves exposure to experiences of true *beauty* through involvement with some area of the arts, nature or life. A discipline of responding with feeling to that which is of greater *quality* is to be cultivated.

Mental—superficial curiosity; inability to concentrate or follow a line of reasoning; a "chatter box" mind; highly responsive to desires and personal interests; conditioned and repetitious. To upgrade the elemental and advance the mental development, the mind must be exposed to universal principles, laws and ideals in a reflective, meditative consideration. Repeated demands to focus on *truth* will quiet the mind, help it to concentrate and teach it to respond to the more inclusive impact of the *universal*.

Just as the elementals have a responsibility to keep the bodies functioning well, so we have the added responsibility of furthering their evolution. A determination to follow the natural laws and the intelligence of nature will go a long way toward that goal.

PART 3

EXPANDING
CONSCIOUSNESS

XIII

MEDITATION

Meditation can be described in so many different ways that one could get the impression that there are many different purposes and processes to meditation. Since there is but one fundamental purpose for living, all else, including meditation, must support that purpose—to integrate personality, Soul and Monad into one whole, functioning, conscious entity. Integration involves three kinds of activities or movements:

Purification—the removal of obstacles such as inertia, glamors and illusions;

Alignment—a mental focus on the objects or objective of union;

Expansion—an extension of consciousness beyond previously defined or experienced limits. There is expansion upwards (personality—Soul—Monad) as well as downwards (Monad—Soul—personality). The lower is the effect seeking to return to and become the higher which is its cause. The higher created the lower but then has to learn to function consciously within its creation until creator and created are one.

Our meditative work is an activity of the personality because that is where we can function consciously. Thus we are attempting to expand our personality to include other states and experiences of consciousness. This movement toward inclusiveness is natural and people try many different ways to do it. Some, like drugs and gangs are not healthy. Other attempts, like spending time in 'nature', joining civic organizations or supporting issues of social concern are more effective. Inclusiveness is an essential process and movement toward wholeness and integration. It is the attaining of the consciousness of another (person, thing, quality, etc.).

For the personality, meditation serves to attain the consciousness of the higher Self. There are four steps to extending one's consciousness to a chosen object/objective:

—examining its form;

—participating in its essential quality;

—being inspired by its purpose;

—identifying with its Soul.

148

The meditation process has several different levels, but there are three in particular that one needs to be aware of: concentration, meditation and contemplation.

Concentration

Meditation is not possible unless one has learned to concentrate or focus the lower mind on the object of meditation. The normal thought-form-making tendencies which are highly colored by conditioning need to be suspended for the duration of the meditation. This can be done only through concentration on a chosen reality which, in meditation, will be a universal rather than a personal reality. What is involved with this meditative concentration is a lower mind focus on a higher mind reality, or the personal mind getting in touch with the 'group' mind. If concentration is very difficult one needs to practice it more, beginning with focusing the mind on physical things and gradually choosing more intangible objects.

It is important to realize that concentration is not only a mental activity, although it is directed by the mind; it is also a Heart activity. Because concentration is also training for compassion—being present with one's Heart—it is only reasonable to include the Heart (and its lower counterpart, the feelings) when developing the ability to concentrate.

Meditation

While concentration maintains a certain distance between the meditator and the object of concentration, meditation brings the two together within the realm of the mind. The lower mind holds itself steady within the light of the higher mind. There it experiences the causes of thought-forms as principles and ideals. There it comes to know the Plan first-hand and be energized by it. There, too, the meditator contacts the Self and experiences a deeper Love, Light and Power than is possible in the personality alone. From this intimate contact with the Soul, the meditator can formulate accurate thought-forms, function creatively and be a positive cause in life.

Contemplation

Through contemplation (one) finds himself able to enter into that silence which will enable him to tap the divine mind, wrest God's thought out of the divine consciousness and to *know*.[1]

---

[1]Bailey, A.A., *A Treatise on White Magic*, 366.

Contemplation may be technically described as the ability of the aligned lower-higher mind to enter the Buddhic/Intuitive realm of divine ideas, laws, and archetypes and the Atmic domain of divine Will and Purpose.

The practice of concentration, meditation and contemplation develop the whole person and produce the necessary integration which leads to Initiation and liberation. *Concentration* links the physical senses, the brain and the lower mind. *Meditation* links all of these to the higher mind. *Contemplation* links all of these to the Buddhic and Atmic Planes. The result is that the Monad now has a suitably coordinated vehicle through which it can express itself in all the worlds of Man.

Meditation is a way of changing the limitations of the personality into the perfections of the Soul, the potentialities becoming actualities and the opposites becoming as one. Meditation is about becoming Truth, Beauty and Goodness—these are the basic potentialities of every person. When this trinity is actualized the result is Unity (integration, inclusiveness, oneness).

Meditation is a way of being present with a greater reality, an at-one-ment with a higher energy. That experience may feel good or appear to be growth-promoting, but by itself it is not complete. In order for energy to actually promote growth it must go through three stages:

—reception
—assimilation
—expression

The meditative experience per se involves reception and assimilation, but not necessarily expression. Expression must be a part of the process if growth is to occur and if over-stimulation and congestion are to be avoided. Expression ought to be:

—a deliberate radiating of the energies contacted before closing a meditation session;

—an effort to act in conformity with the qualities of the energies contacted or to follow the advice of the inner guidance.

Meditative Guidance

Everyone has questions about one's life and the options available at every turn in the road. There are always decisions to make, and a challenge to make wise choices. We can obtain the guidance we seek and get the answers to our questions through meditation. It is the lower mind that asks and the higher mind that responds. When the meditative connection is made the questions are answered. Higher mind is impersonal; it responds with universal principles and ideals. The lower mind has to apply these to the questions to see the answer. It takes a little practice to do this translating but the results are worth the effort.

If one can formulate a question, one has the answer—albeit at another level. The higher mind, which has the answers, is the causal body. It therefore is the cause—direct or indirect—of any question that may arise in the lower mind. We can say that the hidden answer causes the conscious question which elicits a conscious answer.

One of the beautiful things that happens once a person begins to meditate is the unsolicited guidance which starts to operate in a person's life. One is led to the right person, place or things to take the next step. Everything begins to be more meaningfully connected as the Real begins to be the thread tying all experience together. The meditator begins to see that the Soul does control "the outer form, and life and all events."[1]

It is mandatory in this age that all vertical alignment and progress be applied to horizontal action. In the ages past spirituality and materiality were perceived to be separate and mutually exclusive realities. This was a necessary distortion of truth because humanity, previously immersed in material reality, needed to discover spiritual realms and energy to the extreme before being able to synthesize this apparent duality.

We all have, to some degree, been affected by that dualistic approach to wholeness—particularly if we are emotionally polarized, because the astral plane is the plane of duality *par excellence*.

We need constantly to remind ourselves of the need to bring down to earth the energies of the higher realms just as we need to put the lower and separative into the context of the whole.

Meditation practices of the past frequently produced the effect of "taking one up" and leaving one there, further creating a separateness within us. We become used to "dealing with" our problems by escaping to a higher level where they do not exist. In this way we escape from our responsibilities for dealing with our physical bodies and our emotional life.

There is a path of meditation which is very balanced and appropriate—especially for today and for the true disciple who has already achieved a degree of contact with the Soul. It is called *Occult Meditation*.

In this form we contact the higher and progressively bring it into the active, down-to-earth levels of our life, helping us to be more responsible. One of the main emphases in this form of meditation is to contact the higher energies we call virtues, so that these virtues or qualities can be

---

[1]Bailey, A.A., Unification Mantram. *Discipleship in the New Age*, Vol. I, 790.

lived. By bringing their energy into our consciousness we become transformed accordingly.

Suggested Procedure

Meditation is a real art as well as a science. It takes years of practice and experience to master. While many books have been written on the subject, there is no substitute for experience. The books give different approaches with varying motivations and intentions—from stress release to past life recall, from problem-solving to experiencing unconditional love. Some suggestions are not really meditation because they do not expand one. True meditation leads to greater Self mastery; it involves an expansion of consciousness rather than learning a way to satisfy one's desires.

The following procedure works extremely well and helps fulfill all the basic requirements of a well-rounded meditation. It is also open-ended enough to allow for limitless experience.

1. Intend

When sitting down to meditate form a clear intention about what you wish to accomplish. Set the tone and quality by the purity of your motivation. This can be affirmed through an invocation such as The Great Invocation or the Mantram of Unification.

THE GREAT INVOCATION

From the point of Light within the Mind of God
Let light stream forth into the minds of men.
Let Light descend on Earth.

From the point of Love within the Heart of God
Let love stream forth into the hearts of men.
May Christ return to Earth.

From the center where the Will of God is known
Let purpose guide the little wills of men—
The purpose which the Masters know and serve.

From the center which we call the race of men
Let the Plan of Love and Light work out
And may it seal the door where evil dwells.

Let Light and Love and Power restore the Plan on Earth.

MANTRAM OF UNIFICATION
The sons of men are one and I am one with them.
I seek to love, not hate;
I seek to serve and not exact due service;
I seek to heal not hurt.

Let pain bring due reward of light and love.
Let the soul control the outer form,
And life, and all events,
And bring to light the love
Which underlies the happenings of the time.

Let vision come and insight.
Let the future stand revealed.
Let inner union demonstrate and outer cleavages be gone
Let love prevail.
Let all men love.

These are the original versions sanctioned by Lucis Trust, the publishers of the A.A. Bailey writings. Some people have changed some of the words to make the invocations more gender-neutral in their minds, although from an esoteric point of view there is no inherent gender bias.

2. Relax

You know what you are going to do and why you are going to do it. Put it out of your mind now and relax your physical body, quiet your emotions and still the mind. Tensing and relaxing each part of the body may prove helpful, or a simple command to each part such as: "I relax my right foot; my right foot is completely relaxed. I relax my right ankle; my right ankle is completely relaxed," etc. Move through the entire body in this way, relaxing and feeling each body part. With practice the response will be quicker and the state of relaxation deeper. As you narrow the attention so specifically you begin to slow down the brain waves and alter consciousness. The emotions normally quiet at the same time, and the mind generally becomes still as well. However, to insure a good preparatory state for meditation visualize the astral body becoming like a very still lake, with mirror-like quality, reflecting the beauty of the mountains or sky around it. The purpose of the evolved astral body is to serve as a reflection of the beauty of the Intuitive plane of unconditional love. It can only do this once it becomes non-reactive to the lower stimuli. The mental body can be quieted by concentration on some aspect of truth. This may be something related to the truth of one's Self or be the chosen object of focus for the meditation. If an aspect of truth is used for the purpose of concentration, then this part of the procedure ought to be brief. However, concentration can be achieved by going to the next step and concentrating on a seed thought.

3. Choose

Choose an object of focus called a *seed thought*. A seed thought may be a phrase, a word, a quality or a virtue. Since the immediate purpose for most meditators is to integrate with the Soul, it is helpful to meditate on a Soul quality: love, tolerance, courage, beauty, daring, patience, sacrifice, etc.

4. Think

Think about the quality (seed thought). Think what it means to you, how it may be defined, with what it is associated, what its purpose might be, what effects it might have, and whatever you can bring to it from past knowledge. Thinking acquaints you with the "*form*" of the quality.

5. Feel

A few minutes of thought, penetrating as far as the mind can go, then yields to feeling the quality. Feeling involves a more sensuous, emotional, loving and intuitive approach to experiencing the energy of the quality.

6. Become

Feeling, especially at an intuitive level, naturally leads to a union or experience of becoming the quality. Perceiver and perceived merge. There is an identification, an expansion of awareness. Remain with this experience for as long as you experience it. When you begin to leave it by thinking, evaluating, etc. go to step 7.

7. Imagine

Imagine yourself filled with this particular quality and perceive yourself acting in your everyday life with this new quality or new degree of an old quality. Imagine how differently you would feel, what you would be able to do, what your relationships would be like, how others would relate to you, and so on. The more vividly you can imagine it the more likely you are to experience the practical effects of your consciousness experience.

8. Thank and Radiate

Approaching the end of the meditation, give thanks for whatever you have experienced regardless of what it was or whether or not it conformed to your expectations. Then radiate the quality or energy on which you meditated, sending it out to people you may know, to humanity and to all the kingdoms of this planet. Only by sharing can there be reception.

9. Return

Bringing conscious awareness into the present moment of outer reality, become aware of the physical body and environment. Take some deep breaths and open the eyes slowly. Stretching and crossing arms or legs are some ways of bringing one's awareness to a normal waking function. Then happily go about your business.

Meditation Summary

1. Decide on the intention for the meditation with purity of motive.
2. Relax. Enter altered state of consciousness.
3. Choose an object of focus (such as a quality or virtue).
4. Think about it.
5. Feel it.
6. Become it.
7. Imagine yourself acting in your everyday life with this new quality or new degree of an old quality.
8. Give thanks and radiate the quality.
9. Close.

Practical Tips for Meditation

Practice it initially on a regular basis, such as once a day, at the same hour, for a certain length of time.

Choose a location that is quiet and comfortable.

Learn to relax your physical body, to calm your emotions and to still your mind. Pay attention to their needs and then turn your attention to your intention for meditation.

Focusing on the rhythm of the breath helps to establish a conscious inner rhythm as well as to relax the bodies.

Posture during meditation should be comfortable, but not so as to encourage sleep. The preferred position is to sit straight without slouching or drooping the head. If there is a tendency to fall asleep, move forward in the chair, not leaning against the back. The lotus position also has benefits if it can be done easily. Unless the lotus posture is used it is wise not to cross the arms or legs until finished.

It is not important what you wear, though some have a special robe reserved solely for meditation. The advantage to this is the powerful conditioning effects this can have on the subconscious so that it cooperates more readily for the meditation. The small disadvantage is that meditation may become too dissociated from daily living. The clothing ought to be unrestrictive and clean both for comfort and for respect to your Self.

Drugs should be avoided. Different drugs have different effects, from over-stimulating a particular body to tranquilizing the mind. Avoidance of drugs includes abstaining from alcohol and tobacco for a period of time before meditating—the longer the better. While onions and garlic are not drugs, some claim that they stimulate activity on the lower mental body and should be avoided for two hours prior to meditation.

When meditating, have a slight smile on your face—it has a very uplifting effect. A frown creates a depression of vitality in the bodies.

Meditation preceded by elevated or inspirational reading, listening, discussion or singing helps greatly to set the tone and attune the bodies to a higher level.

The time of the Full moon is a marvelous opportunity to serve the planet through meditation. Try to meditate with a group at this time.

XIV

DISCIPLESHIP

A *disciple* is one who follows a particular *discipline*. A discipline is a teaching or instruction; a disciple is a pupil of a teaching. Discipleship in the context of this book, refers to the following of, and dedication to, the Teaching of the 'Great Ones', the Hierarchy, the Soul. It is a state of impersonal, universal allegiance to the common good, serving the Plan as it exists for all kingdoms. A disciple is dedicated to doing the following:

—Implementing the Plan;
—Serving humanity;
—Developing Soul Powers and controlling the tendencies of the personality;
—Following the Soul's instructions regardless of cost or sacrifice.

A disciple is anyone who possesses these orientations to either a lesser or greater degree. The word 'disciple', therefore, applies to such a range of servers from the beginning aspirant up to and including the Christ.

The disciple manifests a different quality of life from that of the average person. There is a movement away from selfish motivation and toward group good. The sense of right proportion develops and demonstrates as giving everyone, including oneself, proper due, as well as giving the group and its potential a greater emphasis. The disciple shows a great deal of sensitivity, but is not easily manipulated by people's expectations or desires because the primary consideration when responding is for the group good rather than for personal satisfaction.

We often think that a disciple follows a Master rather than a teaching. If understood correctly he/she does follow a Master who is the embodiment of the Teaching. The Teaching is a Great Life or a synthesis of many Great Lives. The immediate Master of the disciple is the Soul (Solar Angel) who can say, "I am the Way, the Truth and the Life." From the Christian esoteric perspective this Master is the Christ—the Christ within who is the Soul, but also the Christ who is head of the Hierarchy, "teacher of angels and of men." It is because of this close connection between the Master and the disciple that the disciple sees himself to be an extension—albeit imperfect—of the Master's consciousness. Following a Master is, in reality, following one's Self—not separate and personal, but comprehensive and impersonal.

As the consciousness changes in the disciple to be more impersonal, and thereby more truly loving, there is some struggle and suffering. The lower self is very personal and resists the impersonal. The impersonal and universal are death-threats on the little ego's individual and selfish life. The rebellion from within is usually accompanied by the rebellion from old friends and family who equally dislike one's growing impersonality.

One of the more challenging developments for the aspiring disciple is the use of right speech. Speech is a powerful vehicle of creation, associated with the center of creativity—the throat chakra. Through speech the disciple can use the creative aspect of preserving, strengthening and stimulating. Speech, as creation, is designed to be a vehicle for love. It is not loving to gossip, belittle, criticize or negate. But it is loving to disillusion someone or to expose falseness or unreality of any kind—if it is the right time and the right place. Speech can destroy as well as create. But the destruction must be meaningful and purposeful in order for it to be acceptable. If it clears the way for greater expression of love, it is not only acceptable, but mandatory.

> He who guards his words, and who only speaks with altruistic purpose, in order to carry the energy of Love through the medium of the tongue, is one who is mastering rapidly the initial steps to be taken in preparation for initiation. Speech is the most occult manifestation in existence; it is the means of creation and the vehicle for force. In the reservation of words, esoterically understood, lies the conservation of force; in the utilization of words, justly chosen and spoken, lies the distribution of the love force of the solar system—that force which preserves, strengthens, and stimulates. Only he who knows somewhat of these two aspects of speech can be trusted to stand before the Initiator and to carry out from that Presence certain sounds and secrets imparted to him under the pledge of silence.
>
> The disciple must learn to be silent in the face of that which is evil. He must learn to be silent before the sufferings of the world, wasting no time in idle plaints and sorrowful demonstration, but lifting up the burden of the world; working, and wasting no energy in talk. Yet withal he should speak where encouragement is needed, using the tongue for constructive ends; expressing the love force of the world, as it may flow through him, where it will serve best to ease a load or lift a burden...[1]

---

[1]Bailey, A.A., *Initiation, Human and Solar*, 74.

The transition from the personality-oriented life to the impersonal is a movement of energy focus from the solar plexus to the heart center. What the disciple is basically learning is to love unconditionally, to love without expecting anything in return, to love because it is one's true nature to do so. He learns to love in such altruistic ways not because of desire within, but because of need without. His love is but a response to the need for wholeness that beckons from everyone. Having touched the wholeness of Self within, the disciple can now share a portion of that Self. This is love: the Self seeking itself in and under all forms.

There is a long transitional period for the disciple while he becomes Soul-centered. There is a period of loneliness when one is no longer so concerned about or controlled by the physical, astral or mental bodies, but is not yet balanced within the dynamic inclusiveness of the Soul. That loneliness passes as one becomes more capable and active in group work.

All kinds of difficulties can arise. Patience and endurance are required to weather the storms of life and service. Opposition may come from without, through other people, or from within, through the personality. Excessive self-analysis and hypersensitivity to the criticism of others are common faults. If you experience happiness and pleasure in service be grateful, for all is well.

When a person is truly dedicated to the Master's Will and to serving the Plan, one's aspirations and motivations keep all experiences meaningful. Nothing happens to such a person that is not part of the Plan. Nor is there ever any need to be concerned with one's next step in service. When one is in the right place at the right time with the right motivation and energy—as the disciple is—then the next step *always* reveals itself. What a secure way of going through life! What a marvelous way of eliminating concern and worry! And this way is open to us all.

The discipline of the disciple is no more clearly seen than in a sense of responsibility—a responsibility to others and to the environment by reflecting and standing for the plan of evolutionary progress.

The disciple's responsibility or ability to respond appropriately, according to his level of consciousness, extends in several directions. One needs to be sensitive to the vibrations of the inner Master, to lead a pure life, to be dispassionate, to accomplish one's duty, to take care of the physical body and to understand the nature of the kama-manasic (desire-mind) body.

A disciple is not interested in spiritual advancement or progress. He does nothing to gain merit or reward of any kind. Such considerations are not part of his motivation. Comparison has been replaced by discrimination, which allows him to relax in his knowing and accepting himself as he is. He realizes that if he works hard, has pure motivation, unfolds his intellect, aspires to greater inclusiveness, possesses positive goodwill and opens the inner eye to see reality more clearly, he will progress perfectly.

Most people are incarnated to learn certain qualities, but some have been born with a mission to fulfill. Those who are aspirants on the Path of Discipleship must learn certain qualities to become spiritually attractive and invocative. A more advanced disciple with a mission is noted for the ability to magnetically attract others to himself for their growth or for service, and to invoke, by his life, appropriate blessings on others. This spiritual magnetism is a result of the head and heart of the disciple functioning as a single unit. One then thinks in a loving way and loves in an intelligent manner. This state of integration presupposes the presence of very fine qualities, but also involves the continued perfecting of those qualities essential to discipleship which includes all the Soul qualities, with special emphasis on love, goodwill, service, sacrifice, responsibility, discrimination, humility, simplicity, detachment, serenity, courage, balance, joy and self-control.

Being Soul-centered, the disciple must also have a degree of group consciousness and a willingness to work in group formation. Since discipleship is about service rather than the development of the individual, group formation provides a more effective and potent vehicle through which spiritual energy can be expressed.

Not only are there outer groups with which the disciple is affiliated, but also inner (esoteric) groups, which are part of the consciousness of each disciple. The outer groups apparently were sanctioned by the Hierarchy in 1931 and are still somewhat an experiment in manifestation of the consciousness of the inner groups they represent. The inner groups consist of many individual members, one might say Souls, some in incarnation and some only on the inner planes. These groups are said to be under the direct guidance of a Master and have a common purpose, similarity of vibration (perhaps Ray, such as Soul Ray), and other resonant links.

Successful group work is still, and will be for a long time, a very difficult endeavor. What we will try to do is to maintain sound inner relationships with others in our group even though there may be outer differences of opinion, style or approach. The inner bonds of love must be safeguarded while carrying out one's responsibilities, leaving others to carry out theirs. The tendency to criticize and judge must be constantly watched.

Here are several practical suggestions for anyone aspiring to the path of discipleship:

Practice regular meditation so that the outer vehicles become accustomed to Soul alignment and influence.

Cultivate inner calm and silence, resulting in an inner poise. The balanced stance is a dual activity of holding to the vision and working on the physical plane with concentrated attention. The inner calm is only possible to the extent that the desire nature and the mind can be quieted.

Develop greater purity of motive. Doing the daily review of motives, earlier suggested, would be of great help.

Learn to control thought. Every action, reaction, or dispersion of energy—positive or negative—results from thought. Without this control there is waste and the law of economy is contravened. Controlled thought increases the magnetization of the efforts and the power of their effects.

Fulfill whatever duties and responsibilities you have in your life at any given time. Do not abandon more mundane duties for what you feel might be 'more important' or 'spiritual' responsibilities.

Perfect your domination of the astral.

Learn to work from mental levels.

Stand up for principles without compromise but with patience and love.

> See to it that you deal with patience and forbearance with those of your brothers who choose the lesser principle and the lesser right, who sacrifice the good of the group for their own personal ends or who use unworthy methods. Give to them love and care and a ready helping hand, for they will stumble on the way and sound the depth of the law. Stand ready then to lift them up and to offer to them opportunities for service, knowing that service is the great healer and teacher.[1]

Develop a flexibility and an ability to flow with change. This is possible when we attune to an incoming, or new, energy and adapt to it.

Willingly choose to die so that your love and compassion are selfless and worthy of the beloved.

These approaches to developing a life service, along with those characteristics of disciples previously mentioned, develop one's capacity to be useful to the Great Ones and available for true group work.

---

[1] Bailey, A.A., *A Treatise on White Magic*, 138.

XV

INITIATION

From the perspective of the personality the Soul appears to be relatively perfect on its own plane. After all, it is unconditional Love, it is divine Will and it is intelligent Light; it has also created the bodies of the personality and continues to maintain their life. But there is one area of the Soul's life which is noticeably lacking in perfection—namely, its ability to control matter and transform it into the energy of Soul. Not only is matter of all grades resistant to being transformed into consciousness, it polarizes its resistance in some particular area so as to create a great tension between itself and Soul. The Soul, through time, continues to press itself upon the matter, increasing the tension progressively until the breaking point when the matter yields to consciousness. This breakthrough is an Initiation.

Every Initiation marks an expansion of conscious awareness within matter, a stage wherein the Soul has learned how to control some aspect of matter; or, put another way, where the Soul has been able to express itself more fully through some form or manifestation of itself. Each Initiation, therefore, marks a point of achievement as well as initiating another round of experience and challenge.

An Initiation is a crisis point in the tension between Soul and personality. There is both danger and opportunity—*danger* to the personality, since its transmutation is being demanded (and transmutation implies death to the ego), and *opportunity* to the Soul. Crisis demands decision, so at Initiation the initiate must choose which direction to go—succumb to fear and continued separation or die to love and greater integration.

Every step toward integration is part of the process of simplification. The uninitiated lives in a complex state, with many different views, inclinations, tendencies, desires and thoughts. Integration with the Soul at each Initiation simplifies this complexity by bringing the divergent energies into a comprehensive unity. Universal principles enter into personal experience, so it is the principle which is the unifying and simplifying

162

factor. That which is contrary to the principle is eliminated in the resolution of the tension present at the Initiation.

NINE INITIATIONS

Initiation	Name	Planetary	Solar	Cosmic (Sirian)
1	Birth/Awakening	first	—	—
2	Baptism in Light	second	—	—
3	Transfiguration	third	first	—
4	Renunciation	fourth	second	—
5	Revelation	fifth	third	—
6	Decision/Ascension	sixth	fourth	—
7	Resurrection	seventh	fifth	first
8	Transition	—	sixth	second
9	The Great Refusal	—	seventh	third

A Master "is one who has taken the Seventh Planetary Initiation, the Fifth Solar Initiation, and the first Sirian or cosmic Initiation."[1] At the Ninth Initiation the Master becomes a liberated Monad.

The Eighth and Ninth Initiations are not related to our planetary life so we have no way of comprehending them. For that matter, as individuals we have relatively little understanding of any initiation we have not yet passed through.

The first two are not considered initiations from the Hierarchical point of view. They are considered to be Initiations of the Threshold. Often in esoteric literature (but certainly not always) references to the initiate are meant to imply at least third degree initiation, where there is an awareness and experience of the oneness of life.

Initiates of the first two initiations are usually not very conscious of their true status and have little ability to consciously wield Soul power or force. These are the stages of the *accepted disciple*. Third and fourth degree initiates do work with Soul and through the chakras. Initiates of the higher degrees work with monadic energy and therefore very much through the Antahkarana—especially the group and racial Antahkarana.

Frances Adams Moore makes several interesting observations on both the variations and the common orientations found among initiates. She writes:

> The task of the initiate on the first Ray (Will) is the *preservation of values*; of the initiate on the second Ray (Love-Wisdom) is the *attainment of positivity*; of the third Ray (active intelligent creativity) is *to reach from*

---

[1]Bailey, A.A., *Initiation, Human and Solar*, 18.

here to there; and of the fourth Ray (Harmony through Conflict) is an *arrival at the Will* when conflict moves into its proper place and no longer causes undue concern.

During the early stages of the initiatory process the embryonic initiate works in the *World of Meaning*. After the third initiation work is in the *World of Causes* and, later still, a more advanced state, the initiate works in the *World of Being*.[1]

The Gospel story in the Bible is the story of initiation, Jesus being the initiate; he symbolically enacted the first five planetary Initiations which in the Bible are called:

1. Birth (at Bethlehem).
2. Baptism (in the Jordan River).
3. Transfiguration (on the mountain with Peter, James and John).
4. Crucifixion (on Golgotha)
5. Ascension.

Although it is interesting and even helpful to know what the stages of initiation are and what occurs at each stage, the disciple does not really care what initiation has been attained. The only real concern is a continual striving for greater ability to be an effective instrument for service.

The First Initiation

Having pursued an essentially selfish life for a long period of time, and having found it increasingly wanting, the budding aspirant begins to recognize that there must be something more to life and to oneself. This openness to something greater is what initially sets the stage as an invocation to the Soul for its response. As the Soul responds we have the beginning of the spiritual life. At this stage the physical body and its appetites begin to yield to a higher control. This Initiation involves the physical plane of consciousness although all planes are affected. There is stimulation of the intellect enabling the young initiate to work more on the mental plane in preparation for the Second and Third Initiations. Desire is somewhat superseded by aspiration, although this transmutation will greatly occur at the Second Initiation. At the First Initiation one is consciously and willingly oriented towards the light. One sees a wider world than one's own selfish interests as one becomes sensitive to the Christ life and sensitive to the spiritual consciousness that one finds in one's fellow man. There is a growing sensitivity to possibilities and dimensions beyond the physical, and accompanying this, a sense of

---

[1]Moore, F.A., *The Initiatory Process*, (Meditation Mount, Ojai, CA).

conscious dualism: knowing that there is more beyond the phenomenal world. The First Initiation is really the first major step that an incarnated being takes through the long journey of incarnations. It marks the beginning of a totally new life and mode of living as well as the commencement of a new manner of thinking and of conscious perception.

The First Initiation institutes a new attitude towards relationships, partly due to its own energy and partly due to seventh ray influence. Previous to this Initiation, relationships were determined karmically, physically and emotionally.

> The new relationships...to be increasingly recognized, are subjective and may have but little phenomenal indication. They embrace the recognition of those who must be served; they involve the expansion of the individual consciousness into a growing group awareness; they lead eventually to an eager response to hierarchical quality and to the magnetic pull of the ashram... [It] leads finally to a recognition of the Presence of the Christ and to relationship with Him.[1]

Through Initiation physical sex is seen as a symbol of higher experience; the creative interplay of negative personality with positive Soul. Through the First Initiation the sacral center is most implicated. The energy of this center needs to be transmuted and raised to the throat center, thereby transforming the physical creative act into the creative process of producing the Good, the Beautiful and the True. When the line of light between the brow and crown centers is established the lower energies will be drawn up. This begins to happen at the First Initiation. the seventh ray strongly influences this initiation. Its function is to bring together Soul and body, higher and lower, life and form, Spirit and matter. When the linking has occurred after the First Initiation one can wield energy consciously on the physical plane—and learn to control that energy. (To be conscious of, and to control, are not the same thing.)

Duties

First degree initiates must:

1. Practice meditation.
2. Cultivate a loving heart and express love practically toward all beings.
3. Obey the highest in oneself.
4. Have complete confidence in the power of the indwelling Christ to demonstrate through the personality the life of love.

---

[1]Bailey, A.A., *Rays and Initiations*, 668.

5. Make the life of Christ one's own life—that is, live the life of joy, happiness, sacrifice, service, compassion, etc. which is to live the Soul qualities.

Walking the path of the First Initiation requires initiative, expenditure of energy, overcoming inertia, and the will to exert oneself. It means listening for and obeying the demand of the Soul for a nearer approach to Divinity.

The Second Initiation

The Second Initiation is definitely one of the more difficult periods of the disciple's life. There is testing and struggle that often continues for several incarnations between the First and Second Initiations. There is a great struggle between the personality will and the Soul will. The resolution of this struggle can only come about through gaining control of the emotions, which are personal reactions, and the desire life. This difficult task of transforming the desire nature is made possible by the fact that the first contact with the Shamballa energy of Will now takes place. The special word given at this Initiation is *Express*, indicating the beginning of the ability to express the Will nature of the Monad.

There is much emphasis during the Second Initiation on acquiring very definite qualities rather than on expressing oneself through action. The dominant qualities acquired during this period are love and compassion. There is the transmutation of the solar plexus energies, which are essentially selfish, to the heart energies which are essentially altruistic. This significant movement is only possible through a life of definite discipline on the lower nature to bring a new order and a new way of living into one's personal life. The essential discipline is to cultivate the ability to respond to beauty so that, as the mind learns to grasp greater truth and greater reality, the emotions will be able, naturally and automatically, to respond to the thought-forms. The quality of *devotion* is very important in order to transmute the emotional energies to compassionate heart energies. The object of devotion may be any higher reality. With whatever one devotes oneself to one can develop a discipline of dedication, so that the qualities, the principles and the laws represented by that greater reality can be pursued and followed, thereby establishing a greater rhythm of feeling response.

The dominant personality tendency which needs to be overcome at this Initiation is what we call *glamor*. Glamor can be described as the attribution of false values and exaggerated importance to people, situations, ourselves—virtually anyone or anything. The falseness or exaggeration associated with our perception really creates an inability to see reality and relate to reality clearly, so it is very much connected with illusion. A characteristic of glamor is that there is usually an emotional attachment to it—that is, to the false value or exaggerated importance. Only through careful examination, the development of discrimination, and clear mental vision are we able to perceive glamor for the distortion that it is.

Alice Bailey lists various glamors according to the seven rays. It is interesting to note that the dominant ray in an individual will incline the individual toward particular kinds or groups of glamors.[1] Some of these glamors are:

Ray 1—Power, imposition of authority, ambition, pride, personal strength, conceit, self centeredness, sureness of being right, impatience, irritation, separateness, isolation, aloofness, independence, freedom.

Ray 2—Fear, loneliness, inferiority complex, frustration, depression, sense of futility, self-pity, anxiety, inertia, self-effacement, self-sacrifice.

Ray 3—Being busy, constant planning, scheming, deviousness, manipulation, self-interest, efficiency, preoccupation with material matters.

Ray 4—Beauty, impracticality, vague artistic perception, lack of objectivity, dissatisfaction with existing conditions because of an awareness of what is possible, inner and outer conflict.

Ray 5—Intellectuality, analyzing, dissecting, criticism, insecurity, cold mental assessment, over-emphasis of form.

Ray 6—Personal devotion, possessiveness, fanaticism, rigidity (rigid adherence to an existing form or model), idealism, narrow vision, sentimental attachment.

Ray 7—Law and order, organization, ceremonial and ritual, mystical and secretive, magical powers, psychism, mediumship.

Glamors inhibit us from recognizing reality. Our glamors identify reality as the lower three worlds. To overcome the glamor and the tendency toward glamor it is beneficial to regularly practice disidentification from the three lower worlds and identification with the essence of oneself.

The process goes something like this. Recognizing each of one's bodies, one may say:

"I have a body, but I am not my body. It is a vehicle I use in the outer world for experience in action, but it is not myself. I am not my body."

---

[1]Bailey, A.A., *Glamour, A World Problem*, 120-123.

"I have emotions, but I am not my emotions. They are ways and feelings through which I can experience myself in my environment, but they are not myself. I am not my emotions."

"I have a mind, but I am not my mind. It is an instrument which I control and use to understand life, but it is not myself. I am not my mind."

After the statements of disidentification, one then makes a statement of identification, such as:

"I recognize, accept and affirm that I am the Self, a center of pure self consciousness and will, capable of mastering, directing and using my physical body, my emotions and my mind as instruments of love."

One may also add such affirmations as:

> I am the Soul,
> The Spiritual Self.
> This is the reality in which I take my stand.

Or one may simply use the Soul Mantram:

> I am the Soul,
> I am the Light Divine,
> I am Love,
> I am Will,
> I am Fixed Design.

The Third Initiation

The hardest period in the initiatory journey occurs between the Second and Third Initiations. Frequently there is a great deal of suffering with little inspiration. Occasionally Soul Light enters the mind. This may initially add to the problems but eventually leads to control and freedom.

At the Third Initiation the control of the Soul-illumined mind is finally established. The Soul assumes dominance and does not allow any aspect of the form to control—the limits of form nature are transcended. Theoretically, at least, one has cast off the control of the astral body and nature, but, even at the Third Initiation, full emotional control is not yet established. There has been a transition from an emotional, aspirational focus to an intelligent, thinking focus. Old desires, ancient astral reactions and habitual emotions are still powerful, but the initiate has developed a new attitude toward them.

The Third, Fifth and Seventh Initiations are all related in a special way. They are concerned with freedom—the third, with freedom from the personality; the fifth, with freedom from blindness; the seventh, with freedom from all seven planes of planetary existence. It is not surprising that the Path of Initiation is sometimes called the Path of Liberation. The freedoms that are attained are a result of:

—detachment
—dispassion
—discrimination
—discipline

All of these four techniques or acquired qualities are preceded by a series of disillusionments which, when realized and understood, leave one no choice but to move forward to greater light and greater control.

The first two Initiations can be perceived as self Initiations in that they are taken before the Christ. The Third Initiation is taken before the Planetary Logos, Sanat Kumara. After the Third Initiation one becomes a channel and transmitter of higher energies which enable the Planetary Logos to reach humanity and bring to it fresh life and energy. The work in preparing for the Third Initiation, and the Initiation itself, are purely preparatory to this type of service. The brow center is stimulated, and through this center one begins consciously and creatively to direct available energies towards humanity as a whole. Prior to this Initiation the mind has been very much influenced by conditioning. The mind now is more responsive to ideas, insights, and impulses coming from the Soul; it begins its true task as an interpreter of Divine Truth and as transmitter of hierarchical intention.

The Third Initiation seeks to blend or synthesize dualities—to integrate apparent opposites: human/divine, objective/subjective, inner/outer, primitive/transcendental, personality/Soul. When the dualities are resolved the "new man" shines forth as in the transfiguration. The transfigured being now shines forth in its radiant Soul body.

From the Mount of Transfiguration we must descend into the valley of duty and service. Service leads to increased illumination, and illumination, in turn, finds expression in renewed and consecrated service.

We know relatively little of the nature of Will until after the Third Initiation. From this Initiation onward one demonstrates increasingly and steadily the first divine aspect, that of the Will and of the right use of Power. It is associated with the first ray of Will or Power. The Third Initiation, being the first major Initiation, creates the link with the Monad, the source of Will, Purpose, Life of the individual, and begins the true journey of initiation which is intended to allow complete expression of Monadic Life into outer reality, including in the physical brain consciousness of the disciple.

The third degree initiate transcends the personality and form life and is able to function at will on the buddhic plane, the plane of intuition.

To reveal the world of reality the initiate has obviously overcome illusion. Illusion was previously created by the mind's tendency to misrepresent or misinterpret the truth or higher reality. When the lower mind is unenlightened by the higher mind it always misinterprets and misrepresents the universal, perceiving only in light of the personal and particular. It is not capable on its own of seeing the true nature of reality. At the Third Initiation the higher mind has definitely become active, giving one sufficient light or enlightenment to know the truth about reality without personal distortion. The task now of the lower mind is to create thought-forms for application which are appropriate to the ideals, or principles, laws and archetypes presented by the higher mind.

The Fourth Initiation

The initiate moves in this Initiation from the higher mental plane to the Buddhic/Intuitive level of functioning. The three worlds of human evolution—physical, emotional, and mental—are harmonized with the Buddhic plane. The initiate renounces the lower worlds, the causal body is relinquished, and there is re-enacted within the initiate himself the integration or harmony between humanity and Hierarchy. All the energies of the centers below the diaphragm are renounced for personal use. The initiate now lives for the group, for the planet. One is now a Master of the Wisdom. The initiate lives in the Eternal Now.

With the attainment of freedom from self-interest, which is what true freedom is, the initiate is animated by an engaging purpose. The *unalterable Will* of the Monad is a central fact of brain consciousness now. Prior to this level one is aspiring to greater inclusiveness through the expansion of consciousness. But now the Life aspect supersedes the Consciousness aspect as the primary energy of expression. The liberated disciple perceives the Plan clearly, participates in expressing the energy of Purpose, and actively works at preventing the proliferation of evil.

The Fifth Initiation

The initiate has now become a Lord of Compassion. He has risen "out of the ocean of matter into the pure light of day." At this Initiation the disciple appreciates for the first time the true and complete significance of the will and uses it to relate the head center and the base center, thus completing the integration started at the Third Initiation. The third and highest aspect of the Spiritual Triad, the Atmic plane, is now involved. This is the plane of Will or Spiritual Will. Desire has now been superseded by Spiritual Will. This means that the initiate can now receive inspiration and revelation directly without personal impediment of any kind. This also then enables the initiate to be a clear transmitter of Divine energies. Consciousness is said to be replaced now by the highly suggestive phrase, "universal sentiency and identification." This enables the initiate to experience the full life of Spirit. The Purpose of the Planetary Logos becomes the most dominant factor of the life of the initiate. There is now work to do with the building aspect of Divine Will, aligned with the *Registrants of Purpose* at Shamballa.

The Sixth Initiation

At the Sixth and Seventh Initiation the initiate-Master may be called a Chohan. This is the first of four final solar Initiations, which really are far beyond the understanding of even advanced disciples. This is very much a transition initiation preparing for the final possible planetary Initiation and more importantly the first truly Cosmic Initiation in which one is perfectly free to choose and thus demonstrate essential and gained freedom. This is therefore truly an Initiation of Ascension or the moving into greater worlds. It suggests that everything occurring on this planet is simply preparatory for a greater life. This is a time when one chooses one of the seven paths which lie beyond planetary existence. All of these lead either to the cosmic astral plane or the cosmic mental plane. On the cosmic astral plane there is no glamor, but instead a great vortex of energy—the energy of pure love—under the domination of the Law of Attraction. The seven paths are:[1]

1) The path of earth service. (Cosmic Astral)
2) The path of magnetic work. (Cosmic Astral)
3) The path to Sirius. (Cosmic Astral)
4) The ray path. (Cosmic Mental)
5) The path of absolute Sonship. (Cosmic Mental)
6) The path of training for Planetary Logoi. (Higher Levels of Cosmic Mental)
7) The path the Logos Himself is on. (Cosmic Buddhic)

The paths lead to the mind and heart of the Great Being of Life. All lead the initiate eventually to the Central Spiritual Sun.

---

[1]Cf. Bailey, A.A., *A Treatise on Cosmic Fire*, 1241 ff.

The Seventh Initiation

Relating to the Solar Logos, the seventh degree initiate has the task of bringing the divine aspect of Will into the solar system. He is involved with the development and right use of will. The Chohan enters into the Purpose and into the extra-planetary relationship of Sanat Kumara, Lord of the World. The Law of Synthesis is the controlling universal law for the Master Chohan. The synthesis of the resurrection Initiation is the realization of fulfilled love. Resurrection means to rise to an original state. It implies that the "Son of God has found his way back to the Father and to His originating Source, that state of Existence to which we have given the name Shamballa."[1]

The Eighth Initiation

This Initiation, being so far beyond our attainment, is virtually impossible for us to understand. Frances Adams Moore states:

> At the eighth initiation of *Transition* the Purpose of the planetary activity is revealed and the Initiate-Chohan is aware in a universal sense of all that concerns the sphere of influence of the Will of God, which demonstrates particularly at this initiation. The nature and purpose of duality is revealed.[2]

The Ninth Initiation

The initiate now makes contact with the Central Spiritual Sun and is involved with the nature of Being and Existence. The initiate-Master Chohan has become a liberated Monad.

It is rare for any human to evolve from the earth to the Eighth and Ninth Initiations because the earth is not a sacred planet. The initiate now truly *knows* the one in Whom we live and move and have our being.

Group Initiation

If one did not know otherwise it would be easy to form the impression that Initiation is a solitary path of pursuit. Old style thinking might even go like this: "If I am good enough and nice enough the Hierarchy will recognize me and the Master will reward me with Initiation." Every aspect of this statement is erroneous, even though this kind of thinking is common. The underlying error is the assumption that Initiation is undergone alone. This is an obsolete concept, once promulgated by Hierarchy

---

[1]Bailey, A.A., *The Rays and The Initiations*, 730.
[2]Moore, F.A., *The Initiatory Process*, 15 (Meditation Mount).

to appeal to the aspiring individual disciple. But now the truth, formerly only implied, can now be stated openly: *Initiation is a group event.*

The Soul in its own nature is not a separate reality. It has no individual ambitions or interests as we have in the personality. It is the Soul and not the personality who is the initiate.

It is the Soul-in-form, in incarnated form, that goes through Initiation which marks the stages of ability to bring separate matter (physical, astral, mental) into a non-separate stage of being—the "group consciousness."

Group consciousness transcends personal consciousness and is attained through increased inclusiveness which defines Initiation.

> It dawns on the initiate, as he proceeds from one initiation to another that each time he moves forward on the path or penetrates into the heart of the Mysteries in company with those who are as he is, who share with him the same point in evolution, and who are working with him towards the same goal, that he is not alone; that it is a joint effort that is being made.[1]

Conclusion

The Path of Initiation may appear to be long and arduous, but when compared to the lives we have lived prior to this stage, it is not long and its arduousness is tempered by the growing ability to handle anything that may arise. There is so much joy experienced on this path that even the most painful situations are faced with an eagerness to overcome limitation rather than with former patterns of fear and avoidance. The temporary satisfactions of the previous life are now deep and lasting fulfillment.

MEDITATION ON THE FIVE INITIATIONS
A SYMBOLIC JOURNEY

1. Induction: Induce a very relaxed state of body, emotion and mind.

2. Identify with the Soul Star. The Soul Star is the symbol of the Soul above your head. Center your consciousness within it.

3. Your consciousness is in the light star/Soul star. As the Star of Light you descend from on high and come to rest in a cave. In the cave you see a tiny body beginning to take shape from nothingness. You recognize it as your beginning in human form. As a Soul you send your light into this form, giving it life. It stirs and comes to life. You fuse with it through extending your Love energy. Light and Love imbue the form that is now you. You continue to develop and grow up to 11 years of age. (pause)

---

[1]Bailey, A.A., *The Rays and The Initiations*, 341-342.

4. You leave the cave and walk to a nearby stream that flows at times with great turbulence and violence, and at times with great serenity. You enter the stream to a comfortable depth—up to the level of your heart. You feel cleansed, refreshed, and strengthened. You wash away your desires, and emerge a new person, ready to take on life's challenges with a greater sense of courage. You have grown and matured. You are now 22. (pause)

5. You walk from the stream toward a path that leads up a high mountain. You follow this path and begin to climb, sometimes effortlessly, sometimes struggling over obstacles. There are apparently insurmountable barriers and you don't know how you will ever pass. But you reach deep within and keep your eyes on the top—your goal—and move on. You rest at times to catch your breath and to look at the way you have come. You see the cave in the distance, and the stream below as it winds its way toward the distant horizon and the ocean beyond. You see some of the path you have walked and you know there is progress. As you near the summit there is a great vertical cliff to scale. With determination you proceed and as you set your whole being to the task, you become lighter and lighter. The climb is not as difficult as imagined. You finally arrive at the peak. Standing there with the world below, your body is a body of Light. You are surrounded by Light and filled with Light. You have mastered the greatest challenge of all and surpassed all of your supposed limitations. You are now 33. (pause)

6. There is nothing left to do now, but to re-enter the lower realms, to come down from the mountain top. You begin to descend and find it easy now in your rejuvenated, masterful Soul body. Your challenge before was to release yourself from the pull of the lower forms; your challenge now is to unite with them. As you come back down you become the mountain, you become the Path, you become the rocks, the flowers, the vegetation and the animals. You become all that you encounter and you realize that *you are all that you perceive.* Your essence, your life that flows through you is the same essence and life that flows through all living creation.

Down from the mountain, you enter the inhabited regions of the lower planes where your fellow humans are. You are aware of their problems, their sufferings, their glamors and illusions. But you are no longer trapped by them. You see them and see through them to the essence of love that glimmers in the heart of each. You fuse with that Love; you become one with the inner being of every human until you feel that you are the one humanity. You are ageless.

7. Now as one being, you open yourself to the higher realms again, once more leaving the world behind, now with conscious detachment. As one being, united with all kindred souls, your group light fuses with Divine Light, Divine Love and Divine Will.

Your journey has been a sacrifice and a complete transformation from descent into matter, through redemption of matter, to fusion with the Highest. You are now a complete servant.

8. After some minutes of quiet reflection bring yourself out of this meditation.

XVI

UNIVERSAL LAWS

Most of us live our lives as separate beings, revolving everything around ourselves, accepting with varying degrees of tolerance or intolerance the fact that we have to live with other people, but seldom recognizing the whole of which we are a part, and rarely taking the responsibility of our place in life.

A part has no meaning in isolation. We need to know the whole of which it is an expression. The individual has no meaning by itself; individual existence only makes sense in light of the universal. The personal is empty of significance unless we can grasp the impersonal.

We tend to live our lives on the level of the part, the individual and the personal. We need to recognize the whole, the universal and the impersonal—because these are the causes. The part, the individual and the personal are only the effects.

When we live as effects we have no power, we become victims of other effects. Living attuned to causes, we do have power. It is the power to manifest life and radiate life; the power to choose and align with ultimate purpose; the power to synthesize, unite and fuse; the power to attract and love; the power to distribute energy to fill needs; the power to understand and act intelligently; the power to penetrate identity and express that identity; the power to be who we are as individuals and as universal beings.

What is the whole, the universal and the impersonal? It is always a great Life or a Great Being that enfolds or encompasses lesser lives within it. The universe is one such great Being; so is a galaxy, a solar system, and even our planet. As we learn more about the universe in which we live, we come to appreciate it more. Through astronomy we are learning about the quantitative and even qualitative aspects of these Beings beyond the planet. Through other sciences we are learning about the life of the Being we call our planet, and people are beginning to respond more sensitively to its life.

Through our sciences and observations we discover what we call the *laws of nature*. These laws concern the activities of the Soul of these Beings in form or manifestation. They tell us how the beings function. This helps us get closer to their true nature, but another step must be taken to truly align ourselves, connect with and attune to the life aspect of these greater Beings. We can do this by recognizing our own Soul and Spirit and, by extension, recognizing that the same exists at a more universal level.

Hermes Trismegistus stated a universal axiom: "As above, so below." As we evolve and grow in consciousness we do so from the particular (the below) to the universal (the above). Once we have reached a certain level of growth we grasp the above more directly and can then begin to work on our process of growth toward integration (which is what we live for and what evolution is all about) from above as well as from below. That "certain level" is the level of Intuition which deals solely with universal realities. At that level we can sense the greater Being of which we are a part and begin to identify with it.

Enough members of humanity have reached that universal level so we know something about it. We know that the greater life manifests to us as *Law*, which we call *universal laws*. Even by inference we know that universal laws exist. If there are particular laws, such as natural laws, then universal laws have to exist. If we know the universal laws then we can begin to work with them—with the very energy of the greater Life in whom we live and move and have our being. What we call *Law* is but the spiritual impulse, incentive and life manifestation of a Being. That impulse demonstrates an intelligent purpose wisely directed and based on love.[1]

The universal Being of which we are a part and which conditions all of our experiences expresses itself as three laws:[2]

—Law of Synthesis.
—Law of Attraction.
—Law of Economy.

The Law of Synthesis

The Law of Synthesis operates within all the particulars, the parts and the individuals to fuse, unite and synthesize. The ultimate stages of this process occur at non-material levels. Therefore there is a basic tendency to outgrow form or matter, resulting in death of the form. Forms are always destroyed once the quality is abstracted from them—once we have

---

[1]Cf. Bailey, A.A., *A Treatise on White Magic*, 11.
[2]Cf. Bailey, A.A., *A Treatise on Cosmic Fire*.

derived the meaning from something, that something is no longer necessary and can be let go; or once we have perfected something, it will change. This change implies a destruction, but the destruction occurs only because a new quality of life needs to be expressed.

Obedience is the primary virtue to cultivate to attune to this law. *Will* is the primary faculty to develop. Will is not a mental forcing, but implies a skillful choosing, a decision-making process. What is chosen then dictates what will be attracted under the Law of Attraction. The *lesson* of this law is to discover and follow *right direction*. Intuition needs to be developed to truly understand this law.

> The first of the factors revealing the divine nature, and the first of the great psychological aspects of God, is *the tendency to synthesis*. This tendency runs through all nature, all consciousness, and is life itself. The motivating urge of God, His outstanding desire, is towards union and at-one-ment. It was this tendency or quality which Christ sought both to reveal and to dramatize for humanity.[1]

The synthesis of Soul with Spirit and the synthesis of Soul with matter completes the unification and the desired at-one-ment.

> It is this divine attribute in man which makes his physical body an integral part of the physical world; which makes him psychically gregarious and willing to herd (of choice or perforce) with his fellow man. It is this principle, working or functioning through the human consciousness, which has led to the formation of our huge modern cities—symbols of a coming higher civilization, which we call the kingdom of God, wherein the relationship between men will be exceedingly close psychically. It is this instinct to unify, which underlies all mysticism and all religions, for man seeks even a closer union with God and naught can arrest his at-one-ment (in consciousness) with Deity. It is this instinct which is the basis of his sense of immortality, and which is his guarantee of union with the opposite pole to the personality—the Soul.[2]

Synthesis dictates the trend of all evolutionary processes today; all is working towards larger unified blocks, towards amalgamations, international relationships, global planning, economic fusion, the free flow of commodities everywhere, interdependence, fellowship of faiths, movements based upon the welfare of humanity as a whole, and ideological concepts which deal with wholes, and which mitigate against division, separation, and isolation.

---

[1]Bailey, A.A., *Esoteric Psychology II*, 231.
[2]Ibid., 233-234.

The Law of Attraction

From the Purpose, or the center of Will, there is manifested or radiated the energy of unity. This is the cohesive factor in life which draws all the parts towards a purposeful whole. It gives a direction and meaning to everything. The lower manifestation of that is goal-orientation which fulfills a person's dharma. Dharma can be described as the path of right action determined by an individual's purpose—that is, one's duty to Self and society.

The emanation of the energy of unity is what we call love. Love is the energy that holds all things together, refining them to greater and greater states of integration—always, though, within the framework of purpose. Love without a greater unifying purpose is not love. It is only a pretense or masquerade and, on our part, is a form of selfishness.

In this law we see the quality within attracting the right form and dissolving the form (matter) within it. We see this in relationships where two people who truly love each other, dissolve their separateness into a new whole called a meaningful relationship.

Surrender to that which is sensed as greater or more whole is learned through attunement with this law. Hence, sacrifice becomes a natural consequence and a virtue to be cultivated and constantly practiced.

"Like attracts like" on higher levels. This means that where unity, truth, goodness or beauty exists, all of that which is like it in form or spirit, is attracted to it. If you have unitive motivation, think truthful thoughts, focus on beauty or goodness, you will attract those kinds of experiences. In this process you will let go, or surrender, or eliminate their opposites.

If you have thoughts, feelings or actions which are separative, selfish, ugly, distorted, etc. you will repel unity, truth, goodness and beauty. It is not that you will *attract* the negative, but you will *repel* the positive. The only negative you experience will be that which you create within yourself and project into your experiences.

The Law of Attraction operates because everything is originally *one*. Whenever there are two or more, the principle of resonance causes attraction. The *one* became *two* (yang and yin, male and female). But the male contains the female and the female contains the male, therefore they are attracted to each other and together can return to the *one*.

The Law of Attraction determines how the power of the Spirit attracts matter. It is within the influence of this law that redemption occurs and is possible. Some of the subsidiary laws to the Law of Attraction include:

- chemical affinity   - progress
- magnetism   - radiation
- color   - gravitation
- planetary affinity   - Solar union
- karma   - sex
- the schools

The Law of Economy

This law has to do with the distribution of matter and causes matter always to follow the line of least resistance. It basically gives power to separativeness and allows spirit an avenue to express itself. By itself it leads to complexity, while the other laws lead to increased simplicity. The third aspect of energy, or in this case the third law, must always create a counterpoint to produce a tension for evolution to occur.

The Law of Economy dictates that in the universe all needs are met with the least expenditure of force or energy. On the human level this is done through sharing. Our task is always to devote ourselves to the right distribution of energy and material resources to satisfy and develop the 'ground' for manifestation of consciousness and spirit. To do this we must consider our own life, the lives of people close to us, and the institutional and societal life of this planet. We must also develop the ability to know the difference between true needs and simple desires. This law governs intelligent activity and, therefore, the way we handle matter must be done intelligently. The form of what we do or create is determined by need. We can intelligently determine need, or we can sense or intuit need. If need is known or sensed, and one does not respond to it, a great danger is created for oneself. Knowing need and not responding to it splits us in two, inhibiting the Soul from functioning through its vehicles.

Summary

These three universal laws correspond to the basic trinity of life, the three divine aspects:

    Law of Synthesis—first aspect (Monad, Will, Purpose, Life)
    Law of Attraction—second aspect (Soul, Love, Meaning, Plan)
    Law of Economy—third aspect (Form, Light, Activity, Intelligence)

    The Law of Economy demonstrates as an *urge*.
    The Law of Attraction demonstrates as a *pull*.
    The Law of Synthesis demonstrates as a tendency to concentrate at a
      center, or to *merge*.

XVII

QUESTIONS AND ANSWERS

Q. References to past lives are everywhere. Reincarnation has become as popular as astrology. Is reincarnation an esoteric concept?

A. Reincarnation is an esoteric concept, but it is also a myth. As an explanation of what literally happens in the Soul's journey through time, reincarnation is not to be believed as it is normally discussed. Myths are not intended to explain, but to reveal. They are not meant to be analyzed but to appeal to the heart and to the intuition as revelations of Truth, sensitizing us to some aspect of life's mystery. Myth is symbolic and archetypal. The *concept* of reincarnation as a linear process reinforces psychological fragmentation; the *myth* of reincarnation is intended to show us our connectedness to all life—past, present and future.

The mythical realm is the realm of the Soul where there is no linear time, but time's analogy—duration. In duration the past, present and future co-exist both as actualities and as potentialities or probabilities for manifestation in time. The dual nature of the Soul as both actual and potential suggests that what we experience as an incarnation is one of several possibilities in which we find our focus of consciousness. The many incarnations which we as Souls have, are experienced simultaneously by the Soul. From its perspective outside of time each incarnation is a focal point of consciousness. In each incarnation there is a self-consciousness of individual existence, but because of the existence in time which is characterized by separation, there is no awareness of other incarnations of the Soul. Simply put, each incarnation of the Soul is aware of its own existence only, while the Soul itself is aware of all incarnations at the same time and always.

Once self-consciousness in the individual incarnation expands sufficiently to include more and more Soul awareness (or inclusiveness) there begins to dawn an awareness of one's past and future incarnations. This does not become very accurate until the illusion of separation is overcome through the third initiation. At this stage we begin to see how we, as Souls, are creating everything we are experiencing as a necessity for our greater expression and as a means of providing service to the evolving life of the planetary being.

So what do we make of all the reincarnation stories we hear about, the research that has been done, and our own experiences of what seems to be actual recall of past lives?

There are many possible explanations. Let us briefly explore a few.

1. 'Channeled' past life information or information derived from regression (hypnotic or otherwise) is illusion. It may be a useful illusion or irrelevant illusion. It is useful if it is an accurate or helpful myth to reveal some dynamic or aspect of one's current life. If the subject 're-lives' the past life experience the heart can be healed and the intuition can be opened, enabling one to become more whole in some way. Such an experience should never be taken as literal fact. Too often 'channeled' past life information from another is a projection of the channel's personal myth or imagination and has no real value for the subject.

The level of channeling or regression which yields past life mythology is usually astral and therefore can be useful to reveal karmic realities. Past life regression can be very helpful as a therapeutic process for healing and for karmic balancing. When done at the astral level—which is 98% of the time—it is very personal and hence beneficial from that perspective. The astral is the personal reflection of the intuitive (Buddhic) where the group myth or universal myth exists.

2. There does appear to be some documented cases of past life recall which suggest a possible literal interpretation. These cases are rare and are not provable in a scientific way, but are highly suggestive. [1]

3. There are many feelings people ascribe to possible past lives they have liked. Until we know ourselves more clearly as Soul-conscious beings it is difficult to say with any degree of certainty whether these are what they appear to be or are feelings which come from our participation in the collective consciousness of humanity. In other words, "Am I picking up on 'my' past life or someone else's past life? Or am I, in fact, only projecting some subconscious reality and calling it past life recognition?"

4. The Soul expresses itself in cycles. Because of this, Reincarnation has been called 'the law of cyclic return'. We know little about the cyclic expression of the Soul, but assume that each incarnation is the Soul's

---

[1]Cf. Stevenson, Ian. *Twenty Cases Suggestive of Reincarnation*, (University Press of Virginia, Charlottesville, VA).

manifestation in time. This is probably accurate as far as it goes, but intuitively there seems to be far more to it than that.

We also frequently assume that each successive incarnation is a progression or more advanced expression than previous ones. Perhaps the Soul simply creates a personality life in time to gain the ability to express itself along some particular line (certain combinations of Rays) to redeem matter, and there is no linear progression through time from one incarnation to the next.

It is also possible that the Soul, which in its higher aspects is a group-conscious reality or a 'group Soul,' expresses itself in incarnated form according to a greater reality than individual development. In other words, the reason for our incarnation may have more to do with our essential contribution to the Plan and needs of evolving humanity at any given point in time than with our personal evolution.

5. Reincarnation may be a mythological way of helping us understand or relate to the 'law of cause and effect', commonly known as *karma.*

Karma suggests a continuity of existence which transcends single lifetimes, in which we learn that every cause has an effect. We learn through trial and error initially and through consequences of our thoughts and actions that we are responsible for the way we experience life. We eventually come to appreciate that when we consciously choose to be a cause in alignment with universal laws and principles, the effects produced are beneficial to the common good. The consequences of this responsible way of living bring us into harmony with life. The journey through life teaches us the necessity of being in harmony with all. Since it is not achievable in a single incarnation, the law of karma and reincarnation provide us with a way of understanding the ongoing nature of the quest for harmony.

Q. Now that medical science has developed technology that can artificially 'prolong life', when does death actually occur? In some countries there is legislation that states that death occurs when the heart stops; in other countries death is said to occur when the brain stops functioning. From an energy point of view, can we know the answer to this dilemma?

A. There are three invisible but real links between the body, the Soul and the Monad. They are:

—the life thread
—the consciousness thread or Antahkarana
—the creative thread

The *life thread* emanates from the Monad, the source of individual life. It passes through all the bodies and is the unifying element that keeps them all functioning as a coordinated whole. It is anchored in the physical heart.

The *consciousness thread* also emanates from the Monad. It extends through the Soul to the brain. The lower part of it is between the physical brain and the Soul, while the higher part of it is between the Soul and the Monad. Since the lower part is built of mental substance we currently experience it as the consciousness being developed between the mental unit in the lower mind associated with the brain and the mental permanent atom in the higher mind associated with the Soul. It is also related to the etheric brain and three glands in the head—the pituitary, the pineal and the carotid. When the energy around these three glands is stimulated and connected a triangle is formed and the "third eye" of conscious awareness is born. (The higher part of the consciousness thread between the Soul and Monad is constructed of Buddhic or intuitive substance).

The triple *creative thread* is an extension of the life and consciousness threads and is anchored in the throat center, the center of creative expression. It is said to connect various chakras with the sacrifice, love and knowledge petals.

These petals are symbolically the three tiers or levels of petals of the 'egoic lotus' enclosing the 'jewel in the lotus', representing the Soul. When these petals are unfolding the Soul expresses itself in true creativity.

When the creative thread is not being used the individual is functioning from his conditioned, instinctual nature rather than expressing himself according to his higher nature.

When the consciousness thread is not active or is disconnected a person may be unconscious mentally or physically, but is still alive in the body.

When the life thread is withdrawn by the Monad or the Soul from its connection with the heart, we can say that the person is dead.

When the heart ceases functioning, consciousness and creativity also cease. There is a progression of priority with these three threads. Creativity depends on consciousness and consciousness depends on life.

Q. *One of the expressions that has become so typical in the New Age is: "You create your own reality." So many people use it when they do not want to take responsibility nor help someone in need. "It's their problem," they say. There must be some truth to the saying for it to have become so widespread. If so, what does it really mean?*

A. The Soul, which is our true identity, has created its vehicles, our personality structure, and it continues to influence it throughout our lifetime by its presence of consciousness and qualities. We modify our personality by responding to the Soul's influence or by resisting it. But whatever we do the Soul can work with our choices for ultimate progress and eventual integration.

The Soul's lowest expression on its own plane is the Causal Body, which corresponds to the higher mind. It is cause of all that happens in the personality. This does not mean that it directly causes our resistance to Truth, Beauty and Goodness, but because of its presence with these qualities the personality has something to resist. Without the presence of these we would not be able to resist them; therefore, we can say that the Soul is the indirect cause of our resistance.

When we make choices that are for integration, for awareness, for Truth, Beauty and Goodness, it is Soul directly causing these choices through our personality. On the other hand, when we choose limitation, separation, personal gratification, and when we react emotionally, we are being influenced directly by our conditioning and identification with our personality and its ego. Much of this conditioning is part of our subconscious; we are not even aware of much of it.

How we respond to life's circumstances is therefore determined by our conscious Soul connection or by our largely unconscious personality identification. Since these are the only two possible sources of motivation and perception there is no other way to understand the dynamics of relationships between ourselves and others or between ourselves and our experiences.

To 'create our own reality' does not always mean that you have singly created all the circumstances you experience, but it does mean that *you create the way you experience* the circumstances. Your experience is determined by your perception of the situation. Your responses and reactions are caused by your perception. These in turn, become causes of further experiences. For example, if you have been conditioned by repeated unhappy experiences with teachers in your childhood, and you have done nothing to change that conditioning, you will likely now perceive teachers as people to be avoided or feared. This perception can give rise to fear and rejection whenever you find yourself in a student-teacher relationship, causing you to feel stressed and unable to learn. You might even verbalize mistrust and anger to the teacher, asserting yourself in a way that minimizes the teacher's authority and knowledge so that your ego can feel in control of the situation. The unpleasant situation you are now experiencing is obviously caused by you, even though you will most likely rationalize and justify your reactions as being caused by the present teacher.

Whenever we feel hurt or inadequate in some way in a situation, we know we are identifying with our personality limitations, but rarely take responsibility for these feelings. We do not want to admit that we have created our feelings by our faulty perceptions because then we are also responsible for changing our perceptions. Our automatic (conditioned) response is to blame the other or the circumstances for the way we feel. We rationalize and justify, rather than choose the only healthy alternative there is—namely, Soul perception of the situation. With Soul perception full responsibility is taken, and the power, love and intelligence that comes from that identification enables one to 'create' or experience a different scenario wherein no one gets hurt or feels inadequate in any way. The result of Soul perception is always one of meaningful and loving consequences, causing further purposeful results.

Our purpose for living is to create. When we stop creating we die. And we always have choices for what kind of reality we create and experience.

Q. If the personality is the vehicle of the Soul, when does the Soul enter its vehicles? Some people believe it happens at conception, and others say it happens at birth. Perhaps some clarity from an esoteric perspective would help us resolve the abortion debate.

A. To avoid confusion about the Soul we need to point out that soul is present whenever there is a form of any kind. Soul is that aspect of a thing or person which gives it its particular qualities and characteristics. But there are differences in 'types' of soul—such as mineral soul, plant soul, animal soul and human soul. When the soul is absent there is death or disintegration or simply nothing (no thing, no form).

From the moment of our conception there is, therefore, a soul present, but is it an animal soul or human soul? If it is an animal soul, then as much care and respect must be extended toward the embryo and fetus as one would extend to an animal. But perhaps at the time of conception and shortly thereafter there is only a mineral state of existence, quickly advancing to a 'plant' state, followed by the animal. After all, our physical bodies are essentially animal in nature.

The question of when the human soul enters the fetus cannot be answered with a fixed and pre-determined time. All possibilities seem to exist if we trust the information we have derived from personal regressions conducted by different researchers. Intuitive attunements done in many cases seem to indicate that the same conclusion has to be drawn, making it impossible to legislate when abortion is taking a *human* life and when it is not.

The entire gestation period is a microcosmic recapitulation of the evolution of life and of Man. Each development in the growth of the embryo and fetus has its correspondence in the macrocosm. By correspondence, the third month of the life of the fetus symbolizes the third Root-race, in the middle of which animal man became human, or in other words, individualization occurred. From this fact we cannot conclude anything definitive, but it is highly suggestive of the time when the fetus may be imbued with a human soul.

What distinguishes the animal from the human is the presence of Mind. Geoffrey Hodson describes a clairvoyant observation of the formation of the mental body in a four month old fetus.[1]

At the fourth month the new mental body was seen to be almost colorless, vague in outline, and roughly ovoid in shape. A certain opalescence which suggested color was visible on the surface. The interior revealed the existence of very delicate shades of pale yellow, green, rose, and blue, with violet around the upper part of the periphery. The shades were so delicate as to be suggestions rather than definite colors— foreshadowings of the characteristics of the mental body which was being built.

We cannot draw rigid conclusions from one, or even a few clairvoyant observations, but once again there is some evidence to suggest an evolutionary step is being taken around the third to fourth month.

The final resolution of the abortion dilemma will have to wait for that time when people are sufficiently intuitive and clairvoyant to be able to know with certainty when the Soul enters the body in each case. When that time arrives, and because of the overall human development which will necessarily occur, it is unlikely that abortion will be an issue. Either people will create new life only when they choose or they will come to realize that nothing happens by accident and that every pregnancy is useful and meaningful—for either karmic or dharmic reasons.

---

[1] Cf. Hodson, G., *The Miracle of Birth: A Clairvoyant Study of the Human Embryo*. (The Theosophical Publishing House, Wheaton, IL).

188 Questions and Answers

Q. *Does evil exist? If all is divine either evil does not exist or it is divine too.*

A. Yes, all is divine; the divine is all. But the divine is not only good as opposed to evil, but is both good and evil from an energy point of view. Good is that which is evolutionary, while evil is that which is involutionary (i.e., descending into matter). Both forces or movements are an essential part of the circle of creation. Evolution would not be possible without involution—i.e., good would not be possible without evil. Involution's purpose is ultimate evolution; so, too, evil's purpose is ultimate good. From this point of view we can say, as someone is reputed to have said, "Evil is the length of time it takes for self-perception to occur."

Evil is not wrong or bad in the sense we have been discussing. It is simply an aspect of energy and life, which naturally and eventually synthesizes with its opposite.

But "evil" is sometimes used in a moral sense, and this is where personally biased judgments make absolute pronouncements on the quality and nature of things and people. Morality is dependent upon the consciousness of the individual. "Evil" as a concept should not be used in a discussion about personal morality. The literal meaning of "sin" is more appropriate here, since it means 'to miss the mark,' as in archery.

D. K. shows the meaning of evil as involutionary without passing moral judgment:

> All is evil which drives man deeper into materialism, which omits the
> higher values of living, which endorses selfishness, which sets up barriers
> to the establishing of right human relations, and which feeds the spirit of
> separateness, of fear and of revenge.[1]

The only thing "wrong" with any of these aspects of evil is that they are out of place in a person or group who is on the evolutionary stage of growth, although totally characteristic of the involutionary. But still one cannot be blamed for experiencing and expressing both sides of life's duality while on the road toward integration. Both are divine; both are God.

Q. *I find the references to a hierarchy of beings confusing at times, and sometimes rather disturbing. They remind me of "big brother" keeping tabs on us ordinary people. What is this hierarchy and what is it like?*

A. We live in a time when the concept of *hierarchy* has a negative connotation in people's minds. This is partly due to the fact that a hierarchy

---

[1]Bailey, A.A., *Externalization of the Hierarchy*, 187.

implies a vertical structure of authority, with the 'higher'-positioned imposing their will upon those lower on the totem pole. Hierarchy is therefore associated with suppression, imposition and abuse of power. We have witnessed this throughout human history, especially in political and religious organizations in society.

At this time in our history there is a reaction to past abuse along with an emphasis on individual human rights and even glorification of the individual. This is a necessary swing of the allegiance pendulum away from mass consciousness to self-consciousness. The balance has not yet been struck. While this movement is happening there is another consciousness development occurring wherein the balance will be attained through group consciousness. This is the next step. In order to take this step in a social sense there must be a shift from vertical structures to horizontal structures in which every participant is honored, respected and perceived as equal.

None of these developments—all of which are in fact furthering human evolution—are contrary to the idea of a hierarchy of beings. We find the model of hierarchy in nature and since we humans are part of nature we are part of some type of hierarchical structure.

In nature that which is 'higher' is that which is greater and more inclusive, and therefore more powerful. In nature the greater and more powerful always has the function of supporting and giving meaningful fulfillment and direction to that which is lesser in some respect. If we look at the hierarchy of the kingdoms of nature we can readily see how this hierarchical principle applies. The plant kingdom is responsible for the mineral kingdom. It carries out this responsibility partly by consuming the mineral kingdom for its own nourishment. We can say that the mineral kingdom evolves into the plant kingdom by becoming it through the plant's assimilation. In much the same way the animal kingdom relates to the plant kingdom, consuming it and transforming it into itself.

The human kingdom's place in the hierarchy of kingdoms is somewhat unique because the human has all three of the lower kingdoms within its physical body. That which distinguishes the human from these other kingdoms is the presence of MIND. Therefore, the human responsibility is mentally and practically to have a proper supporting relationship to the physical body and the physical world.

Another factor of human uniqueness among the kingdoms is the presence of the fifth kingdom within the human constitution. The fifth kingdom is the *kingdom of Soul*. This kingdom is made up of incarnated souls in human form as well as souls who have evolved beyond the human kingdom. Within the human being the Soul has the responsibility for the mind and lower nature. It is slowly consuming all of that within the human being which is not Soul, thereby transforming it into the highest possible state or quality. This process is one of dying on the part of the little ego to become the big Ego (i.e., the Soul)—more inclusive, more powerful, more qualitative, more conscious and more alive.

On a larger scale, those Souls who have surpassed the human kingdom have the responsibility for the meaningful direction of all humanity. They have a planetary relationship, and therefore are often called the *Planetary Hierarchy*. They are also called by such names as *Planetary Masters, Hierarchy of Masters, Mahatmas, Masters of the Wisdom, Spiritual Hierarchy, Great White Lodge, Elder Brothers,* the *Great Rishis,* the *Communion of Saints,* or simply *Hierarchy*.

Because of the qualitative development of these Beings they are referred to as *Masters of Compassion* which suggests how they relate to the human kingdom. The essence of the Soul within each of us is LOVE, and the essence of the fifth kingdom is also LOVE expressed as compassion. The Soul within does not impose its will upon the personal will, but lovingly presents its will for mental consideration. Conscience is its voice until there is sufficient awareness present in which the person can more consciously know the will of the Soul or the Divine Will.

On the planetary level the Hierarchy compassionately presents the Divine Will as the *Plan* for humanity to follow. Those humans who have developed sufficient mental sensitivity respond to this Plan by grasping its universal ideals and by seeking to implement them. Those who have developed intuition become embodiments of the Plan, and with great love and compassion for their fellow humans they become the true leaders in the various fields of human endeavor, inspiring human effort for cooperation and advancement.

In order for humans to become part of the next kingdom we must become group conscious and within that state embrace individual self-consciousness as well as mass consciousness.

In this hierarchy of relationships there is perfect order, the greatest possible potential for growth, and absolutely no disregard for any level of being. There is no imposition of any kind, only inspiration, guidance, direction and meaning for every human being. Let us develop our hearts and minds so that we can be touched by the compassion and wisdom that are constantly being extended toward us.

FOR FURTHER INFORMATION

Andrew Schneider lectures and conducts seminars at his retreat center in British Columbia, Canada, and around the world. If you would like to contact his office about presentations or information about his tapes or newsletter, he can be reached at:

Other Dimensions Services
Box 2269
Salmon Arm, B.C. V1E 4R3
Canada
Telephone/Fax: (604) 832-8483

ABOUT THE AUTHOR

At the age of 14 Andrew Schneider entered a seminary to study for the Roman Catholic priesthood with the Benedictine monks. He trained with them for five years, gaining a solid academic grounding for his later studies, developing a deep spirituality and learning to live in a disciplined way. He then joined an Italian missionary order with hopes of serving in Africa. He took his philosophical studies in Connecticut before spending three years in Italy where he took a year's novitiate and two years of theology in Rome. His studies covered such wide-ranging fields as logic, epistemology, eight languages, sacred archeology, existential and scholastic philosophy, primitive art, moral theology, classical music and the history of English literature.

Andrew left the religious life after eleven years to pursue studies in psychology at the University of British Columbia, followed by a year at Simon Fraser University. Andrew then worked for four years as a teacher and school counselor in the B.C. school system.

The year 1974 marked the beginning of a totally new orientation.

Prior to 1974 Andrew's work included: teaching children of all ages; teaching at colleges; translating books and magazine articles for publication; counseling; working with the poor, sick, physically and mentally handicapped and emotionally disturbed; writing a newspaper column on metaphysical subjects; founding and operating a school for New Canadians; and teaching Yoga.

Since 1974 Andrew has worked full time in the metaphysical field. He has founded two schools for esoteric studies in Canada and Europe, and is currently creating another school for the development of consciousness and the training of world servers. He has taught nearly 4,000 classes, seminars and workshops. He was once described as "a teacher of teachers and a healer of healers." His sensitivity and warmth, his deep interest in people's well-being, his vast knowledge combined with intuitive perception, and his ability to express complex ideas in clear, simple language make him a respected teacher and sought after speaker.